The Internet Angel

THE BEST 1000 DISCOUNT WEBSITES

Annie Challis

Back cover photo by Michael Maples

This book is designed to provide accurate and authoritative information in regards to the subject matter and websites mentioned herein. However, although the information in the book was verified at the time of going to print the author and publisher cannot take any responsibility for any changes in the products, services or actual availability of the websites. It is sold with the understanding that the author is not engaged in rendering legal, accounting or other professional services. If legal or expert advice is required the services of a pfrofessional person should be sought.

Requests should be sent to info@TheInternetAngel.com

A portion of the profits for this book will go to various homeless charities.

CONTENTS

Home Exchange
Home Insurance Comparison
Internet Superstores
Job Search
Language Translators
Legal Help
Life Insurance Comparison Quotes
Mortgage Rates Comparison
Photo Sharing
Real Estate Valuations
Recipes
Reference and Research
Renters Insurance
Screen Savers
Search Engines
Shipping Rates
Sitters
Shopping Clubs
Social Networking
Swap Sites – Books, CDs, DVDs and Games
Swap Sites – General
Utilities
Web Hosting
Website Templates

ACKNOWLEGMENTS

I can't say "thank-you" enough to my dear friend Maggie Wilde for her editing and words of wisdom, not to mention laughs at my late night spelling mistakes. Thanks to all my family and friends for passing on websites they use and recommend and for putting up with me having my head in the Internet for the past months; to my brother Michael for all his support and love, and to Kristen and Lee for their encouragement and sharing the tricks of the trade with me, and for living in wine country.

For Charlie, Jake, Millie and Eve.

INTRODUCTION

This book is a guide for everyone who wants to find bargains and discounts in online shopping – and who doesn't need a good deal these days?

When you Google a product or service you're looking for you'll find a bewildering number of websites. Google 'discount perfume' and you'll get over 2 million hits. 'Discount cell phone plans'? Well over 50 million sites claim the best deal.

I've taken the guesswork and drudgery out of your web searches by researching and testing the sites and have whittled them down to the **best of the best** in each category.

The sites you'll find here are extremely diverse and cover the gamut of products and services available online, from A to Z and everything in between. From auto parts to zebra skin rugs, I've got you covered. You'll easily find the best deal going on the web for whatever you're searching for without clicking through endless dead ends.

Before you commit to an expensive cell phone, mobile broadband or DSL contract, check out what's available in your area on the easy-to-decipher sites I've selected.

You'll be able to find the best credit card rates and bank rates with one click, which can result in years of savings.

I've also listed travel sites, auction sites, comparison-shopping sites and sites with free coupons and weekly discounts, as well as the very best research sources and charitable 'daily click' giving sites.

Perhaps best of all I have researched each site for those difficult-to-find fine print details: customer service numbers, payment options, shipping options and return policies.

Even when you're in a hurry you'll never again have to settle for less than the best deal for you!

You will also have access to TheInternetAngel.com whch will be updated regularly to keep pace with the ever-changing deals available on the web.

ACCESSORIES

EYEGLASSES

www.eyebuydirect.com

1-800-439-6628

Huge savings on prescription eyeglasses and sunglasses starting at $7.99 including free case and cloth.

Shipping: free over $99 or choose at checkout
Return Policy: Within7 days, restocking fee 50%. Contact customer service for RMA#.
Payment Options: Major credit cards, PayPal, Google Checkout.

Similar sites:

www.sunglasswarehouse.com

1-800-559-4209

Shipping: Free on orders over $25 or choose at checkout
Return Policy: Contact customer service within 365 days of purchase for RMA#
Payment Options: Major credit cards

www.39dollarglasses.com

1-800-672-6304

Shipping: Choose at checkout
Return Policy: Contact customer service for RMA# - 30% restocking fee applies.
Payment Options: Major credit cards and Western Union.

ACCESSORIES

www.framesdirect.com
1-800-248-9427

Shipping: Choose at checkout
Return Policy: Within 30 days – 50% restocking fee
Payment: Major credit cards

www.goggles4u.com
1-800-540-3198

Shipping: Free
Return Policy: 50% restocking plus return at your cost.
Payment Options: Major credit cards

www.thriftyspecs.com
1-800-962-5003

Shipping: Free
Return Policy: No return for custom items.
Payment Options: Major credit cards and PayPal.

HANDBAGS

www.bagsbuy.com

1-888-200-8414

Handbags, backpacks, luggage and accessories with hundreds of brands and designer names.

Shipping: Free standard or choose at checkout
Return Policy: Go online for return slip within 90 days. Free return shipping.
Payment Options: Major credit cards, PayPal, Bill Me Later, eBill Me, Google Checkout, Western Union

Similar sites:

www.handbagheaven.com

1-800-259-8487

Shipping: Free or choose at checkout
Return Policy: Contact customer service within 45 days for RMA#
Payment Options: Major credit cards, PayPal, Google Checkout

www.baghaus.com

1-877-861-7257

Shipping: Free on orders over $100 or choose at checkout
Return Policy: Return within 30 days of purchase. Return slip in package.
Payment Options: Major credit cards

www.ebags.com
1-800-820-6126

Shipping: Choose at checkout
Return Policy: Go online within 60 days of purchase for return form.
Payment Options: Major credit cards and PayPal

LUGGAGE

www.luggageguy.com

1-800-971-4920

All types of luggage sets, wheeled suitcases, carry-ons, garment bags, tote bags, satchels, duffels, business bags, laptop bags and travel accessories.

Shipping: Free or choose at checkout
Return Policy: Go online for RMA# to return.
Payment Options: Major credit cards and PayPal

Similar sites:

www.luggageonline.com

1-888-958-4424

Shipping: Choose at checkout
Return Policy: Go online within 30 days for UPS return label.
Payment Options: Major credit cards and PayPal

www.discountluggage.com

1-800-551-7090

Shipping: Choose at checkout
Return Policy: Contact customer service within 30 days for RMA# to return unused items.
Payment Options: Major credit cards

HATS

www.lids.com

1-888-564-4287

All styles of hats – from latest fashion hats for men, women and kids to sports fans hats for MLB, NBA, NFL, NHL.

Shipping: Free on orders over $50 or choose at checkout
Return Policy: Within 30 days refund with original receipt. No refund on custom-made items.
Payment: Major credit card

www.blankcaps.com

1-800-332-6576

blankcaps.com have an assortment of caps suitable for customizing.

Shipping: Choose at checkout
Return Policy: with 10 days must call for RMA#
Payment Options: Major credit cards and money orders

GLOVES

www.backcountryoutlet.com

1-800-409-4502

Gloves of all kinds for all occasions – lightweight, mittens, ski, fleece, snowboard gloves and glove liners – for men, women and children.

Shipping: Free on orders over $50 or choose at checkout
Return Policy: 100% satisfaction guaranteed, go online to get RMA#
Payment: Major credit card and PayPal

JEWELRY

www.shopdi.com

1-800-515-3935

All kinds of jewelry with diamonds and other gemstones including bracelets, pendants, earrings, necklaces and rings of all types. And best of all they have an outlet section with discounted jewelry up to 50% off.

Shipping: Free
Return Policy: Contact customer service within 30 days for RMA# and return instructions.
Payment Options: Major credit cards and PayPal

www.greatjewelrybargains.com

1-504-615-1191

This site is a liquidation outlet for manufacturers, suppliers, wholesalers and retailers. All types of jewelry and loose diamonds.

Shipping: Choose at checkout
Return Policy: Mandatory to get RMA# on their website link. Must be returned in the same condition as received.
Payment Options: Major credit cards and PayPal

www.outletjewelry.com

1-800-238-3642

Discounts of 35-75% off retail prices everyday on bracelets, earrings, necklaces, pendants, rings and loose diamonds.

Shipping: Choose at checkout
Return Policy: 100% guaranteed. Call customer service within 30 days.
Payment Options: Major credit cards

Similar sites:

www.palmbeachjewelry.com

1-866-804-3745

Shipping: Choose at checkout
Return Policy: No return on personalized items. Other returns within 90 days of order with return slip in order.
Payment Options: Major credit cards, Easy Pay Plan

www.jewelryandwatches.org

1-866-216-1072

Shipping: Choose at checkout
Return Policy: Read details for return and insurance. Return within 30 days
Payment Option: Major credit cards

www.goldspeed.com

1-800-465-3340

Over 20,000 items of jewelry up to 78% off retail prices. They also will buy your old jewelry.

Shipping: Free
Return Options: Contact customer service within 30 days for RMA# Restocking fee may apply.
Payment Options: Major credit cards, Bill Me Later, PayPal, Layaway, Wire transfer

DIAMONDS

www.buydiamonddirect.com

1-800-886-1515

Largest selection of loose diamonds on the internet. Choose by the carat size, color, clarity, price range, cut grade and shape.

Shipping: Choose at checkout.
Return Policy: Must call customer service with 10 days to get RMA#.
Payment Options: Major credit cards, cashiers check and money order.

Similar sites:

www.goldenmine.com

1-800-619-1375

Shipping: Free on orders over $100 or choose at checkout.
Return Policy: Within 60 days of purchase return with original invoice.
Payment Options: Major credit cards

www.usadiamonds.net

via email

Shipping: Free
Return Policy: Within 30 days
Payment Options: Major credit cards, PayPal and Google Checkout.

UMBRELLAS

www.umbrellas.com

1-800-676-1578

Hundreds of colors and styles of umbrellas for men, women and children, including doormen umbrellas, sports, beach and personalized.

Shipping: Choose at checkout
Return Policy: Contact customer service within 6 days for RMA#. 15% restocking fee applies.
Payment Options: Major credit cards and online checks

UNIFORMS

www.bestbuyuniforms.com

1-800-345-1924

Many types of uniforms for career, formal wear, work uniforms, chefs, nursing and medical, police and security, aprons, spa and salon, housekeeping and maids uniform. Plus all types of overalls, smocks and lab coats. All at 50% below competitors prices.

Shipping: Choose at checkout
Return Policy: Contact customer service within 15 days for RMA#. 20% restocking fee applies
Payment Options: Major credit cards

www.uniformwarehouse.com

1-800-243-6805

Every type of uniform for the restaurant including aprons, formal, chefs apparel and shoes.

Shipping: Choose at checkout
Return Policy: Within 60 days. Return slip in order with pre-paid label.
Payment Options: Major credit cards

www.uniformcity.com

1-866-814-0145

Scrubs for men and women and shoes and stethoscopes, including some clearance items

Shipping: Choose at checkout
Return Policy: Return slip in package, must be within 30 days
Payment Options: Major credit cards

Similar site:

www.allheart.com

1-800-323-2329

Shipping: Some free or choose at checkout
Return Policy: Within 30 days in original condition
Payment Options: Major credit cards

WATCHES

www.discountwatchstore.com

1-866-371-2330

Discountwatchstore.com carries many brand name watches including Invicta, Seiko, Orient, Omega, Tag Heuer and more at discounted prices.

Shipping: Free on orders over $130 or choose at checkout
Return Policy: Mandatory to get RMA# from customer service if not satisfied. Unused only
Payment Options: Major credit cards and PayPal

www.authenticwatches.com

1-805-823-8888

Guaranteed authentic big brand name watches at lowest prices. Tag Heuer, Breitling, Gucci, Cartier, Rolex and loads more.

Shipping: Choose at checkout
Return Policy: Contact customer service within 30 days for RMA#. 10% restocking fee applies.
Payment Options: Major credit cards, PayPal and wire transfer.

www.jewelryandwatches.org
1-866-216-1072

Brand name jewelry and watches at discount prices

Shipping: Choose at checkout
Return Policy: Read specific details regarding return and insurance
Payment Options: Major credit cards and PayPal

AUTOMOBILES

AUTO PARTS

www.autoanything.com

1-800-874-8888

Any accessory you might need for your car saving up to 40% off list price. Products include car covers, mats, chrome accessories, seat covers, grills, exhaust systems and loads more.

Shipping: Free
Return Policy: Contact customer service within 30 days for RMA#. Some items are subject to 15% restocking fee.
Payment Options: Major credit cards, PayPal, Bill Me Later and Western Union.

www.autopartswarehouse.com

1-800-913-6119

A very easy to use website – put in the make and year of your vehicle and find the replacement auto part you are looking for.

Shipping: Free on orders over $50 or choose at checkout.
Return Policy: No hassle. Email customer service for RMA# within 30 days of purchase date.
Payment Options: Major credit cards, Bill Me Later, Google Checkout and PayPal.

Similar sites:

www.partsgeek.com

1-800-541-9352

Shipping: Choose at checkout
Return Policy: Contact customer service for RMA#.
Payment Options: Major credit cards

www.partsamerica.com

1-877-808-0698

Shipping: Choose at checkout
Return Policy: In original condition only and within 30 days.
Return slip on back of original invoice.
Payment Options: Major credit cards

www.partstrain.com

1-888-251-1214

Shipping: Choose at checkout
Return Policy: Within 5 days call customer service for RMA#.
25% restocking fee applies.
Payment Options: Major credit cards and Bill Me Later

TIRES

www.tirerack.com

1-888-541-1777

Put in your vehicle details and follow questions about weather etc. and they will suggest the right tires for your car.

Shipping: Choose at checkout
Return Policy: Call customer service for RMA# within 30 days Unused tires only.
Payment Options: Major credit cards

www.discounttire.com

1-800-774-6560

Enter your vehicle details as promoted and they show sizes that fit your car. Then enter your zip code and they will show you a store to pick them up and have them installed.

MIRRORS

www.discountautomirrors.com
1-888-231-5293

Easy to use – select make, model and year and the mirror you need will come up at low prices.
Shipping: Choose at checkout
Return Policy: Go on to site within 30 days to fill out RMA form. 10% restocking fee applies.
Payment Option: Major credit cards

BABY NEEDS

CLOTHES, BEDDING, DIAPERS

www.babyage.com

1-800-222-9243

Thousands of products at extremely competitive prices including car seats, strollers, clothes, toys, nursery, diapers, feeding and more. They also have an outlet section for even better prices.

Shipping: Flat rate $9.99 or free on orders over $75.
Return Policy: Contact customer service within 30 days for RMA#.
Payment Options: Major credit cards and PayPal.

www.diapers.com

1-800-342-7377

diapers.com carries baby needs including diapers, nursing needs, bath and skin products, nursery, toys and clothes. And they have a Green Baby section with organic food, cleaning items and much more.

Shipping: Free on orders over $49
Return Policy: In unopened packages within 30 days of sales order.
Payment: Major credit cards and PayPal

www.BunnyCreek.com

1-888-383-4825

Clothes for baby and toddlers, bedding, diapers, baby gifts, gift baskets and nursery décor all at discount prices of up to 70% off regular retail prices.

Shipping: Flat rate – free with online coupon code
Return Policy: Call for RMA# and details vary.
Payment: Major credit cards and PayPal

www.babymallonline.com

1-845-473-6780

babymallonline.com has bedding, bath linens, bibs and potties at highly discounted prices.

Shipping: Free on orders over $100 or flat rate
Returns: Within 30 days of order if unused and unopened.
Payment: Major credit cards and PayPal

www.babydirect.com

1-800-717-1163

Nursery furniture, bedding, car seats, strollers and more.

Shipping: Choose at checkout
Return Policy: Within 30 days of purchase go online to customer service for RMA#. Restocking fee applies.

www.babytobee.com

via email

babytobee.com is a great site for mothers and fathers-to-be with loads of free stuff for the coming baby. Free diapers, discount coupons and samples, tons of free offers and subscriptions to top baby magazines, health advice and gift vouchers.

COUPONS FOR FREE BABY STUFF

www.babiesonline.com

www.babytobee.com

www.planningfamily.com

www.bestfreestuffonline.com

www.surebaby.com

www.coolsavings.com

www.babyzone.com

www.freestuff4baby.com

BIRTH ANNOUNCEMENTS/STATIONERY

www.shutterfly.com

1-888-225-7159

Upload your baby pictures to create your own birth announcements, baby books, shower invitations, baptism and christening invitations, scrap books and more.

Shipping: Choose at checkout
Return Policy: Go online for a return form within 30 days of order.
Payment Options: Major credit cards

Similar sites:

www.storkie.com

1-800-771-7867

Shipping: Choose at checkout.
Return Policy: No returns on personalized items
Payment Options: Major credit cards

www.tinyprints.com

1-877-300-9256

Shipping: Choose at checkout
Return Policy: No returns on personalized items
Payment Options: Major credit cards

www.simplybabystuff.com

1-800-274-4282

Shipping: Choose at checkout
Return Policy: No returns on personalized items, other items
call customer service, restocking fee applies.
Payment Options: Major credit cards

DISCOUNT DESIGNER WEBSITES

DESIGNER CLOTHES

www.Bluefly.com

1-877-258-3359

One of the most highly recommended sites for designer clothes for men and women, shoes, handbags and accessories at huge discounts. Gucci, Fendi, Stella McCartney, Tory Burch, Dolce Gabbana and many more. You should go on daily as they have unexpected offers with even bigger discounts, and contests to win items on the site.

Shipping: Flat $7.99 or choose at checkout
Return Policy: Returns can be made within 90 days with enclosed prepaid label in order
Payment Options: All major credit cards

www.Hautelook.com

1-888-547-8438

Hautelook.com call themselves a fashion club and they are. They have access to the latest premium fashion and luxury lifestyle brands discounted at up to 75% off regular retail prices.
Sign up to become a member and they will send you an email announcing the brand and the start date of the sale. The sale usually lasts 12-48 hours, but get in quickly as they have a limited number of each item. Merchandise ranges from designer clothes for men and women to shoes, handbags, lingerie, kids clothes and jewelry.

Shipping: Choose at checkout
Return Policy: Returns available on most items. Check with
customer service.
Payment Options: All major credit cards

www.Ruelala.com

1- 888-992-5252

Ruelala.com is an exclusive invitation only membership site
that is a private sales boutique selling premier brands at
discounted prices.   Membership is free and members can
invite friends to join.
Once signed up you will receive an email with details of
each sale and the start date and how long it will last. Get
on quickly as the number of items is limited.

Shipping: Choose at checkout
Returns: 30 day return policy. Use UPS return label in order.
Payment Options: All major credit cards.

www.shopittome.com

via email

Shopittome.com is like an online personal shopper. You fill in
a profile of your brand preferences and size and each day
or week – up to you – they will send you a "salemail" email
with a list of items for sale and the stores they are available
from. You click and are through to that retailer. They include
Calvin Klein, Nordstrom, Banana Republic, Victoria's Secrets,
Dolce and Gabbana, Nike, Louis Vuitton and many more.

Shipping, returns and payment varies for each store.

www.giltgroup.com

via email

Invitation only members shopping sales for men's, women's and children's designer fashions and luxury brand items up to 70% off retail prices. Once signed up as a member you will receive an email to inform you of the brand, when the sale starts and an advance preview. The sale last for 36 hours and is first-come first-served.

Shipping: Choose at checkout
Returns: 14 day return policy on apparel and shoes and store credit only. No returns on other items. See web site.
Payment Options: All major credit cards.

Similar Sites:

www.biliondollarbabes.com

www.ideeli.com

www.topbutton.com

ALERTS

For the style conscious sign up and get a free daily alert or weekly email from these sites to keep you up-to-date and aware of sales, services, travel, gadgets, nightlife, restaurants and bars in your area:

www.dailycandy.com

www.julib.com

www.yelp.com

www.topbutton.com

www.thrillist.com

www.style.com

www.shopintuition.com

www.shopkitson.com

www.urbandaddy.com - for men

www.vitaljuicedaily.com - for wellness

www.idealbite.com - for green living

DESIGNER HANDBAGS

www.efashionhouse.com

1-702-448-8639

efashionhouse.com is a blog that is connected to five web stores where you can shop using one card and checkout process (see websites below). They all have the best prices online for authentic designer handbags and purses. Designers include Chanel, Chloe, Hermes, Fendi, Gucci, Prada and many more. Get an extra 10% off your first order when signing up for email newsletter.

Shipping: Choose at checkout:
Return Policy: No hassle return policy for store credit less shipping. Must call or email customer service within 48 hours for RMA#. Unused items only.
Payment Options: Major credit cards and Layaway

www.luxuryvintage.com

www.valuebag.com

www.brandboutique.com

www.Italysoutlet.com

www.designersLA.com

Similar site:

www.indulgencehandbags.com

1-206-508-1443

Shipping: Free
Return Policy: Contact customer service within 24 hours to get RMA#
Payment Options: Major credit cards and Google Checkout.

DESIGNER SUNGLASSES

www.designersunglassesdiscount.com

1-347-702-7780

Authentic designer sunglasses at up to 50% off retail price. Many well known brand names like Chanel, Dior, Gucci, Prada and many more.

Shipping: Free ground or choose at checkout:
Return Policy: If not satisfied return unused with 5 days of purchase. 20% restocking fee applies.
Payment Options: Major credit cards

www.coolframes.com

1-888-293-4755

100% guaranteed authentic designer sunglasses including Prada, Gucci, Ralph Lauren and loads more. 100% price matching policy plus specials and promotions.

Shipping: Standard shipping free or choose at checkout.
Return Policy: Return within one week of delivery. 20% restocking fee applies.
Payment Options: Major credit cards.

ENTERTAINMENT

BOOKS

www.amazon.com

via email

Amazon.com is the best worldwide website for any and almost every book you could want from bestsellers to out of print. They have customers selling books too, so if it's not in their warehouse there is a good chance that you can get it through a third party. Well laid out and easy to use website. Also has self-publishing and many other non-book items.

Shipping: many options including sign up for Amazon Prime for small annual fee and get free 2-day shipping on all orders. Supersaver shipping – free on orders over $25. Otherwise depends on size and weight.
Return Policy: Easy return within 30 days. Label in original package or contact online returns center.
Payment: Major credit cards, Amazon Visa card, online check, Bill Me Later, web certificates.

www.bookcloseout.com

1-888-402-7323

One of America's largest sellers of bargain books. All books are new and unread they are just publishers sell-offs, so may have a remainder mark on them. Hundred of books, many varied subjects.

Shipping:. Choose at checkout
Return Policy: No returns
Payment: Major credit cards

Similar sites:

www.yourdiscountbookstore.com
1-310-514-2971

Shipping: Free on orders over $25
Return policy: Within 7 days, restocking and postage fees apply
Payment: Major credit cards

www.booksamillion.com
1-800-201-3550

Shipping: Free on orders over $25 or choose at checkout
Return Policy: No returns.
Payment: Major credit cards and PayPal

www.barnesandnoble.com
1-800-843-2665

Shipping: Free on orders over $25 on eligible items or choose at checkout.
Return Policy: Within 14 days, some non-book items not returnable
Payment: Major credit cards and PayPal

www.borders.com
1-800-770-7811

Shipping: Free on eligible items or choose at checkout.
Return Policy: Within 30 days with return label enclosed in order.
Payment Method: Major credit cards and Bill Me Later

CAMERAS

www.abesofmaine.com

1-800-992-2237

The average purchase on this site saves the buyer approximately 50% off recommended retail price. Cameras, photography equipment, video, TV, home audio and a clearance department with even bigger discounts.

Shipping: Choose at checkout
Return Policy: Contact customer service within 30 days to get RMA#. Some items excluded from refund. Must be original packaging.
Payment Options: Major credit cards and money orders

www.adorama.com

1-800-223-2500

Everything photographic from cameras and accessories to software. Also a used equipment department.

Shipping: Choose at checkout
Return Policy: Contact customer service within 7 days for RMA#. Some items non-refundable.
Payment Options: Major credit cards.

www.bhphotovideo.com

1-800-606-6969

All photography needs and video and digital imaging, plus used equipment department

Shipping: Choose at checkout
Return Policy: Must contact customer service within 15 days for RMA#.
Payment Options: Major credit cards, PayPal, Bill Me Later, Google Checkout and wire transfer.

CELLPHONES

www.wirelessemporium.com

1-714-278-1930

wirelessemporium.com has all types of cell phones, PDAs and factory direct accessories including batteries, chargers, faceplates, ring tones etc. Up to 75% off retail prices.

Shipping: Free shipping on all orders
Return Policy: Within 30 days of receipt. Contact via email for RMA#
Payment Options: Major credit cards, Bill Me Later and Google Checkout

Similar sites:

www.shopcell.com

1-718-853-2355

Shipping: free on orders over $125 or choose at checkout
Return Policy: All sales are final unless damaged.
Payment Options: Major credit card or money orders

www.wirefly.com

1-888-947-3359

Shipping: Options at checkout
Return Policy: Can request full refund if not satisfied contact customer service within 15 days for RMA#
Payment Options: Major credit cards

www.cellphoneshop.com

1-866-381-1670

Every kind of accessory you might need for every brand of cell phone. Chargers, faceplates, batteries, cases, cables, Bluetooth and much more.

Shipping: Free on order over $30 or choose at checkout
Return Options: Contact customer service within 14 days of receipt.
Payment Options: Major credit cards.

www.cellularoutfitter.com

1-714-278-1930

Shipping: Choose at checkout
Return Policy: Email customer service within 30 days for RMA#
Payment Options: Major credit cards and Google Checkout

CDs, DVDs AND BLU-RAY

www.deepdiscount.com

1-800-264-5076

Dedicated to providing the lowest price online shopping for DVD's, CD's, Blu-ray and video games.

Shipping: Free
Return Policy: Within 30 days of ship date in original packing. May be subject to restocking fee.
Payment Method: Major credit cards and Bill Me Later

www.cduniverse.com

1-800-231-7937

cduniverse.com sells domestic and imported music CD's, DVD's and video games.

Shipping: Choose at checkout
Return Policy: Within 30 days of order in unopened original packaging. Return slip is sent with order.
Payment Method: Major credit cards, PayPal, Google Checkout and Bill Me Later

HOLIDAY DECORATIONS

www.bettyschristmashouse.com

1-815-673-5824

Christmas lights of all colors and shapes, pre-lit trees, wreaths, garlands, ornaments and topiaries. They also have light arrangements for other occasions like Valentine's Day, Easter, Halloween, St. Patrick's Day, sports occasions and weddings.

Shipping: Calculated at checkout
Return Policy: If not satisfied you must call for RMA#
Payment Options: Major credit cards

Similar sites:

www.holidaydecorationsdirect.com

1-888-478-4603

Shipping: Some free or choose at checkout
Return Policy: Contact customer service within 30 days for RMA#. 10% restocking fee applies.
Payment Options: Major credit cards, PayPal and Google Checkout

www.christmasdepot.com

1-877-353-5263

Huge discounts on Christmas lights, decorations and artificial trees.

Shipping: Choose at checkout
Return Policy: Within 30 days call customer service for RMA#
Payment Options: Major credit cards

www.christmaslightsetc.com

1-866-962-7382

Shipping: Free on tree over $95 or choose at checkout
Return Policy: If not satisfied, contact customer service within 30 days to get mandatory RMA#. 10% restocking fee plus shipping charges apply.
Payment Options: Visa and Mastercard.

COMPUTERS

www.newegg.com

1-800-390-1119

newegg.com has more than 25,000 computers, hardware, software and other consumer electronics in stock. Mac and P.C.

Shipping: Choose at checkout
Return Policy: Mandatory to request RMA# online within 15 days of order.
Payment Method: Major credit cards, Bill Me Later and PayPal.

www.outletpc.com

1-702-262-7968

Wholesale prices on computer systems and parts. They also sell used and refurbished computers.

Shipping: free on orders over $150 or choose at checkout.
Return Policy: Download RMA# request form from website.
Payment Method: Major credit cards and PayPal.

www.pcexchange.com

1-866-540-9999

pcexchange.com has high quality reliable refurbished used and off-lease computers and laptops provided with one full year warranty.

Shipping: Choose at checkout
Return Policy: Within 30 days of purchase. Email customer service for RMA#.
Payment Method: Major credit cards, PayPal and Google checkout.

www.tigerdirect.com

1-800-800-8300

As well as a huge store of electronics TigerDirect.com has an enormous amount of refurbished laptops and computers.

Shipping: Choose at checkout
Return Policy: Go online within 30 days of purchase for RMA#
Payment Options: Major credit cards, eBillMe, PayPal, BillMeLater, Google Checkout.

COMPUTER ACCESSORIES

www.supermediastore.com

1-626-363-1490

Flash memory, hardware, CD/DVDs and many more accessories.

Shipping: Choose at checkout
Return Policy: Contact customer service within 30 days for RMA#
Payment Options: Major credit cards

Similar site:

www.keenzo.com

1-516-280-3767

Shipping: Choose at checkout
Return Policy: Contact customer service within 3 days for details
Payment Options: Major credit cards

WEB CAMERAS

www.geeks.com

1-760-726-7700

Web cameras, surveillance cameras and accessories.

Shipping: Choose at checkout
Return Policy: All sales final
Payment Options: Major credit cards and PayPal

www.radioshack.com

1-800-843-7422

Shipping: Choose at checkout
Return Policy: Contact customer service within 30 days for RMA#
Payment Options: Major credit cards and PayPal

ELECTRONICS

www.thetechgeek.com

1-510-226-9918

thetechgeek.com has over 30,000 items online making the site a one-stop solution for electronic goods. Computers, Wii, videos, tv's, audio, home electronics, batteries, office equipment, iPod depot and much much more.

Shipping: Choose at checkout
Return Policy: Get hassle-free RMA# online within 30 days of invoice date.
Payment Method: Major credit cards and PayPal

www.tigerdirect.com

1-800-800-8300

tigerdirect.com has electronics of all kinds including camcorders, digital cameras, pgs, tv's projectors, home theatres, mps players, computers, DVD players, speakers, phone systems, satellite radio and more.

Shipping: Flat rate $2.99 on orders over $150 or choose at checkout.
Return Policy: Within 30 days go online to get RMA# and details of how to return.
Payment: Major credit cards, PayPal, Bill Me Later, eBill Me and Google Checkout.

www.4electronicwarehouse.com

1-866-224-6171

Everything you need for home including televisions, ipod accessories, cameras, remote controls and many accessories.

Shipping: Free on order over $75 or choose at checkout
Return Policy: Contact customer service.
Payment Options: Major credit cards, PayPal and Google Checkout

www.ecost.com

1-877-888-2678

ecost.com has deals on everything electronic. Customers can sign up for Platinum Premium for $39.95 for free shipping, additional discounts and newsletter.

Shipping: Choose at checkout
Return Policy: Call customer service to obtain RMA# within 30 days of invoice.
Payment Options: Major credit cards, Bill Me Later and PayPal

Similar sites:

www.outlettrail.com
1-800-882-5916

Shipping: Choose at checkout
Return Policy: Go online within 15 days of purchase for RMA#
Payment Options: Major credit cards and PayPal

www.geeks.com
1-760-726-7700

Up to 80% discount on a huge variety of televisions and computers.

Shipping: Choose at checkout
Return Policy: All sales final. Defective returns only within 30 days.
Payment Options: Major credit cards, PayPal and Bill Me Later

www.teptronics.com
1-866-859-1800

Affordable audio and video products for home, mobile and car.

Shipping: Choose at checkout
Return Policy: Contact customer for RMA# within 15 days of delivery
Payment Options: Major credit cards and PayPal.

Similar sites:

www.bestpriceaudiovideo.com

1-800-982-8273

Home audio, tv's, video, cameras, GPS navigation systems, Bluetooth products and much more.

Shipping: Choose at checkout
Return Policy: Go online for RMA# form
Payment Options: Major credit cards

www.beachcamera.com

1-800-572-3224

Shipping: Choose at checkout
Return Policy: Contact customer service within 30 days for RMA#. Some exceptions.
Payment: Major credit cards and PayPal

MAGAZINE SUBSCRIPTIONS

www.magazines.com

1-800-624-2946

The oldest and largest website for discount magazine subscriptions covering a multitude of subjects all with huge savings.

Shipping: Free on all magazines
Return Policy: 100% satisfaction guaranteed
Payment Options: Major credit cards

Similar magazine subscription sites:

www.magazineline.com

1-800-959-1676

Shipping: Free
Return Policy: Cancel at any time and you will receive refund for remaining order.
Payment Options: Major credit cards or get billed later.

MUSICAL INSTRUMENTS

www.musiciansfriend.com

1-800-391-8762

All types of guitars, amps, keyboards, brass, woodwinds, drums, percussion, karaoke systems, lighting and audio systems and so much more. The also have a 45 day lowest price guarantee, so if you find an item cheaper at a US authorized dealer call customer service and they will refund.

Shipping: Free on orders over $99 or choose at checkout
Return Policy: Satisfaction guaranteed, if not pleased within 45 days, get RMA# from customer service for refund.
Payment Options: Major credit cards, PayPal and Bill Me Later.

Similar sites:

www.cheapbandgear.com

1-330-494-2100

Shipping: Choose at checkout
Return Policy: Return within 15 days unopened after getting RMA# from customer service. 20% restocking fee applies.

www.music123.com

1-888-566-6123

Shipping: Choose at checkout
Return Policy: Contact customer service within 45 days for RMA# - some items non-returnable.
Payment Options: Major credit cards

www.instrumentalsavings.com

1-800-860-4077

Shipping: Free on orders over $199 or choose at checkout.
Return Policy: Contact customer service within 30 days for RMA#. 18% restocking fee applies.
Payment Options: Major credit cards, PayPal and Google Checkout.

www.musicianshut.com

1-866-835-1611

Shipping: Choose at checkout
Return Policy: Contact customer service within 30 days for RMA#. 10% restocking fee applies.
Payment Options: Major credit cards, PayPal and Google Checkout.

PARTY SUPPLIES

www.discountpartysuppliesfavors.com
1-866-272-9897

Everything you need for any occasion – party accessories, decorations, hats, masks, novelties, gift baskets, inflatable items, noisemakers, paper goods and personalized items.

Shipping: Choose at checkout
Return Policy: Contact customer service within 14 days for RMA#.   No returns on costumes and wigs.
Payment Options: Major credit cards

www.celebrateexpress.com
1-800-424-7843

Everything for kids theme parties and costumes for baby, kids, teens and adults.

Shipping: Choose at checkout
Return Policy: Return within 14 days unused. Some items excluded from returns so contact customer service.
Payment Options: Major credit cards

Similar sites:

www.partycelebration.com

1-888-727-8911

Shipping: Choose at checkout
Return Policy: All sales final
Payment Options: Major credit cards

www.epartyunlimited.com

1-800-726-6698

Shipping: Choose at checkout
Return Policy: Download return form from website. 10% re-
stocking fee applies.
Payment Options: Major credit cards and PayPal

www.pinatas.com

1-866-746-2827

Huge choice of piñatas, including personalized ones and
for any party occasion. Plus costumes and party supplies.

Shipping: Choose at checkout
Return Policy: Within 5 days of receipt of order
Payment Options: Major credit cards and PayPal

COSTUMES

www.buycostumes.com
1-800-459-2969

Adult and kids costumes, party supplies, accessories, make-up, hats, wigs, masks and pet costumes.

Shipping: Choose at checkout
Return Policies: Within 14 days .
Payment Options: Major credit cards

Similar Site:

www.starcostumes.com
1-888-573-4594

Shipping: Choose at checkout
Return Policy: Call customer service within 10 days for RMA#. Unused items only. 20% restocking fee applies.
Payment Options: Major credit cards and Google Checkout

www.spirithalloween.com
1-866-860-0155

Shipping: Choose at checkout
Return Policy: Instructions on the back of original invoice
Payment Options: Major credit cards

www.costumecraze.com
1-888-922-7293

Shipping: Choose at checkout
Return Policy: All sales final
Payment Options: Major credit cards and PayPal

www.costumes4less.com
1-888-726-7886

Shipping: Choose at checkout
Return Policy: Contact customer service within 10 days for RMA#
Payment Options: Major credit cards, PayPal and Google Checkout.

POSTERS

www.allposters.com

1-888-654-0143

Over 500,000 posters and prints with topics like fine art, photography, vintage, travel, animals, movies, music and more.

Shipping: Choose at checkout
Return Policy: 100% satisfaction guaranteed. Must contact customer service within 30 days of delivery for RMA#.
Payment: Major credit cards and PayPal

SOFTWARE

www.buycheapsoftware.com

1-888-999-02611

Every type of software at hugely discounted prices.

Shipping: Free on orders over $200 or choose at checkout
Return Policy: Go online within 10 days of purchase for
RMA# to return item in original unused condition.
Payment Options: Major credit cards

www.childrenssoftwareonline.com

1-866-774-8505

Educational software with fun graphics and animation.

Shipping: Free
Return Policy: In original condition within 30 days of pur-
chase. 20% restocking fee applies.
Payment Options: Major credit cards, PayPal and check.

TICKETS

The following are useful sites for tickets for concerts, sports, theatre, Las Vegas, Broadway, Nascar and more. You can also sell tickets that you have and cannot use on these sites.

www.Stubhub.com
1-866-788-2482

www.ticketliquidator.com
1-800-456-8499

FOOD AND BEVERAGES

BAKERIES

www.1-800-bakery.com

1-800-287-9870

This site offers baked goods sent overnight from their New England bakery packed to arrive just as it left. They offer breads, pastries, and cakes for any occasion, cookies, desserts and gift baskets, plus special diet items.

Shipping: Overnight
Return Policy: If not satisfied 100% money back guarantee.
Payment: Major credit cards

www.bakemeawish.com

1-888-987-9474

Gourmet cakes for any occasion in a variety of flavors.

Shipping: Fedex
Return Policy: No returns
Payment Options: Major credit cards

CHOCOLATE AND CANDY

www.worldsfinestchocolate.com

1-888-821-8452

A family owned company based in Chicago with home-made chocolate, gift items and personalized items for all occasions.

Shipping: Choose at checkout
Return Policy: 100% guaranteed. Call customer service
Payment Options: Major credit cards.

www.candydirect.com

1-619-216-0016

All types of candy from bubble gum to jelly beans to chocolate. Packed to order in personalized tins or boxes.

Shipping: Free on order over $75 or choose at checkout
Return Policy: Some items non returnable, check with customer service.
Payment Options: Major credit cards

www.thepopcornfactory.com

1-888-216-0235

Popcorn either for the family or fancy flavors and fancy containers for gifts for every occasion.

Shipping: Choose at checkout
Return Policy: Contact customer service
Payment Options: Major credit cards

COFFEE AND TEA

www.coffee.org

1-800-344-2739

coffee.org has well-known brands of coffee like Starbucks, Seattle's Best, Maxwell House and more. Whole beans, ground, instant, organic, hot chocolate and many types of teas.

Shipping: Calculated at check out
Return Policy: Call customer service for RMA#
Payment Options: Major credit cards and PayPal

www.coffeeforless.com

1-888-893-7593

Offers many coffee brands including Folgers, Dunkin' Donuts and pods. Teas like Tetley, Lipton and Tazo, and hot chocolate. Also available is a selection of coffee and espresso machines, creamers, sweeteners and more.

Shipping: Free with orders over $50 or choose at checkout
Return Policy: Within 30 days call customer service for RMA#. Items in original condition. 20% restocking fee on some items.
Payment Options: Major credit cards

GOURMET FOOD

www.wholesalegourmet.com

1-877-451-6724

Wholesale prices for goodies such as candy, chocolate, cookies, beverages, cheese, snacks, condiments, crackers, nuts, pasta, cakes and ready-made meals.

Shipping: Choose at checkout
Return Policy: Unopened within 3 days of purchase. 20% restocking fee applies.
Payment Options: Major credit cards.

WINE AND ALCOHOL

All sites selling wine and alcohol of any kind will not sell to anyone under 21 years of age, and insist that any deliveries are received by an adult over 21 years old with photo id.

www.mywinedirect.com

1-866-330-9463

They take pride in finding hidden gems from small vineyards. Free membership to their wine club on first purchase.

Shipping: Free on all orders.
Returns Policy: Will replace any damaged items.
Payment Options: Major credit cards.

www.BevMo.com

1-877-772-3866

BevMo.com is the number 1 beverage website. It's the on-line home of BevMo who have over 90 stores in California and Arizona.
BevMo sells wines, spirits and beers. They have a rewards program with an extra 5% savings once you have spent $250.

Shipping: Choose at checkout
Return Policy: Varies - contact customer service
Payment: Major credit cards

Similar sites:

www.winebuyer.com

1-800-946-3937

Shipping: Choose at checkout
Return Policy: Will replaced damaged items.
Payment Options: Major credit cards

www.winelibrary.com

1-888-980-9463

Shipping: Choose at checkout
Return Policy: Call customer service within 30 days
Payment Options: Major credit cards

GREEN SECTION

BABY

www.babyearth.com

1-888-868-2897

Green living for everything for baby. Products include clothes, bath needs, feeding, toys, learning, nursery, car seats and much more, including a clearance section.

Shipping: Free on orders of $99 or choose at checkout
Return Policy: Must contact customer service within 30 days for RMA#
Payment: Major credit cards

www.betterforbabies.com

1-877-303-4050

Natural and organic baby products – diapers, training pants, clothes, baby slings and sleep accessories.

Shipping: Choose at checkout
Return Policy: Contact customer service within 30 days for RMA#
Payment Options: Major credit cards and PayPal

CARBON FOOTPRINT

The following sites show you how to reduce your negative impact on the environment.

www.carbonfootprint.com

www.sustainourplanet.com

www.lowimpactliving.com

www.cleanair-coolplanet.org

www.terrapass.com

www.begreennow.com

www.stopthejunkmail.com

www.catalogchoice.org

www.nma.org

CLOTHES AND JEWELRY

www.patagonia.com

1-800-638-6464

Patagonia.com has great clothes for men, women and kids from outdoor sportswear to boxer shorts. They strive to use recycled products like soda bottles and worn-out fabric in their polyester, recycled nylon and organic cottons. Even their range of footwear is made from recycled products.

Shipping: Choose at checkout
Return Policy: Return slip included in order. Send with original invoice for refund.
Payment Options: Major credit cards.

www.missionplayground.com

1-888-954-9367

Eco-friendly clothes for men, women and children. 1% of profit goes to non-profit organizations that share the site's passion for the environment.

Shipping: Choose at checkout
Return Policy: Return in traceable shipping method.
Payment: Major credit cards

www.greenappleactive.com
1-866-516-3180

Sells active wear including t-shirts and sweat clothes made from bamboo mixed with organic cotton. Very soft and silky.

Shipping: Choose at checkout
Return Policy: Contact customer service within 30 days for RMA#
Payment Options: Major credit cards

www.thegreenloop.com
1-503-236-3999

Stylish but environmentally correct apparel and accessories. All brands use eco-friendly sustainable materials.

Shipping: Choose at checkout
Returns Policy: Return in original condition within 30 days. Must call customer service for RMA#.
Payment: Major credit cards, PayPal

www.nau.com
1-877-454-5628

Men's and women's clothes made from environmentally-friendly fabric and fibers.

Shipping: Free on orders over $150 or choose at checkout
Return Policy: Return details in order or contact customer service.
Payment Options: Major credit cards

www.stewartbrown.com

via email

Women's clothes made with organic cotton fabric, natural fiber knitwear and cashmere from the undercoat combed from goats of Outer Mongolia.

Shipping: Choose at checkout
Return Policy: Contact customer service within 5 days for RMA#
Payment Options: Major credit cards

JEWELRY

www.greenkarat.com

1-877-330-4605

Eco-jewelry made to order from recycled gold specializing in wedding and commitment rings.

Shipping: Choose at checkout
Return Policy: Return within 30 days, no returns on custom-made items.
Payment Option: Major credit cards

COSMETICS AND SKINCARE

www.terrafirmacosmetics.com

1-866-869-1346

All products are non-animal tested, no chemical dyes, no artificial fragrances and uncoated minerals. Facial care, babycare, footcare, brushes, skincare and mineral makeup.

Shipping: Choose at checkout
Return Policy: Within 45 days return unused items in original packaging.
Payment Options: Major credit cards

Similar sites:

www.skinbotanica.com

1-877-682-3553

Shipping: Free on orders over $49 or choose at checkout.
Return Policy: Within 60 days. Go online for RMA form.
Payment Options: Major credit cards

FOOD

www.sunorganic.com

1-888-269-9888

Everything organic – baking goods, breakfast foods, coffee, dried fruit, nuts, oils, wine, Asian specialties and gift packs.

Shipping: Choose at checkout
Return Policy: Check for damage within 7 days of delivery and contact customer service if not satisfied.
Payment Option: Major credit cards and check

Similar sites:

www.diamondorganics.com

1-888-0674-2642

Shipping: Overnight – choose at checkout
Return Policy: If not satisfied return with note giving reason.
Payment Options: Major credit cards

www.healthytraders.com

1-888-392-9237

Great source for natural food, cookware, supplements and books

Shipping: Free on many items. Choose at checkout
Returns Policy: Must contact customer service within 14 days for RMA#. 20% restocking fee applies
Payment: Major credit cards, PayPal

www.simply-natural.biz

1-888-392-9237

Site with many things organic including natural foods, cook-
ware, clothing, supplements and snacks,
Shipping: Choose at checkout
Return Policy: Contact customer service within 14 days if
not satisfied. Restocking fee applies.
Payment Options: Major credit cards

KIDS AND BABY CLOTHES

www.sckoon.com
via email

High quality 100% organic clothes, toys and diapers. Plus accessories for the pregnant woman.

Shipping: Choose at checkout
Returns Policy: Return slip in order, must return with 20 days in original condition. 15% restocking fee applies
Payment: Major credit cards

Similar site:

www.pureandhonestkids.com
1-866-294-0126

Shipping: Free on orders over $75 or choose at checkout
Return Policy: Use return slip in order with 14 days of purchase.
Payment Options: Major credit cards

www.katequinnorganics.com
1-888-952-4206

Shipping: Free on orders over $100 or choose at checkout
Return Policy: Within 30 days of purchase in original condition
Payment Options: Major credit cards

www.hazelnutkids.com

1-888-869-1901

Natural, earth friendly wooden and organic cotton toys for kids and babies.

Shipping: Flat rate of $5.99
Return Policy: Contact customer service within 30 days for RMA#.
Payment Options: Major credit cards, PayPal and checks.

HOME ACCESSORIES

www.greenandmore.com

1-877-473-3616

Loads of green items for the home – recycling bins, energy use monitors, household cleaners, humidifiers, light bulbs, attic covers, tankless water heaters, compost bins, and so much more.

Shipping: Free on orders over $50 or choose at checkout
Return Policy: Contact customer service within 30 days of purchase. Restocking fee may apply.
Payment Option: Major credit cards and PayPal

www.3rliving.com

email

Home décor and lifestyle products. Great gift items under $10. Stationery, solar powered accessories, candles, books, cookware and more.

Shipping: Choose at checkout
Return Policy: E-mail customer service for RMA# within 30 days of purchase.
Payment Options: Major credit cards

www.theshadestore.com

1-800-754-1455

Custom-made solar shades for energy efficient benefits.

Shipping: Free or choose at checkout
Return Policy: No returns on custom-made unless manufac-
turers error.
Payment Options: Major credit cards

www.airandaqua.com

1-866-380-2782

All types of water and air purifiers.

Shipping: Choose at checkout
Return Policy: Contact customer service with 30 days. 15%
restocking fee on all returns.
Payment Option: major credit cards and PayPal

BEDDING

www.kushtush.com

via email

Healthy and eco-safe organic bedding including comforters, mattresses, blankets, sheets and pillowcases plus everything for baby beds.

Shipping: Free on order overs $100 or choose at checkout
Returns Policy: Must contact customer service for RMA#.
Payment: Major credit cards, PayPal

ALLERGY CONTROL ITEMS

www.allergybegone.com

1-866-234-6630

Products to keep allergies under control including bedding, air cleaners, dehumidifiers, vacuum cleaners, air filters, water filtration and more. Plus weekly special offers and gifts.

Shipping: Choose at checkout
Return Policy: Contact customer service with 30 days for RMA#
Payment Options: Major credit cards

HOUSEHOLD PRODUCTS

www.gaiam.com

1-877-989-6321

Home cleaners for laundry, pest control, and general household cleaners plus lighting, water and more. Also organic workout wear and yoga clothing.

Shipping: Choose at checkout
Return Policy: Return slip in order
Payment Option: Major credit cards and Bill Me Later

Similar sites:

www.ecowise.com

www.mrsmeyers.com

www.holycowstore.com

www.seventhgeneration.com

www.greenandmore.com

Below are sites that will help you find eco-friendly products for the home:

www.ecopaint.com
www.greenlivingideas.com

PET SUPPLIES

www.robbinspetcare.com

1-877-542-0880

Pet care accessories, herbal supplements, dental care, collars and leashes, apparel, beds and much more.

Shipping: Free on orders over $75 or choose at checkout
Returns Policy: Must be unopened and returned within 30 days of delivery. Return slip in order.
Payment: Major credit cards, PayPal

Similar sites:

www.ecosumo.com

via email

Eco-friendly selection of accessories, pet care, toys, treats and clean- up items for your pets.

Shipping: Choose at checkout
Return Policy: Contact customer service within 30 days for RMA#
Payment Options: Major credit cards

www.shop.ecopetlife.com

via email

Shipping: Choose at checkout
Return Policy: Within 30 days except for special orders.
Payment Options: Visa, MasterCard or PayPal

RECYCLING

Below are sites for you to find recycling in your area for everything.

Just put in your zip code and they will let you know the addresses to drop off old cell phones, televisions, CDs, video games, inkjet cartridges, computers, office machines, electronics, paint and more.

www.earth911.com

www.mygreenelectronics.org

www.recyclingnearyou.com

www.recyclingplaces.com

www.recyclingcenters.org

www.electronicsrecycling.org

www.ewastedisposal.net

www.kab.org

USEFUL SITES

www.greenlivingideas.com

1-877-548-4733

Provides ideas, tips and help to improve the environmental sustainability of every aspect of your life.

Similar sites:

www.ecomall.com

www.greendealsdaily.com

www.pristineplanet.com

www.greenpeople.com

www.seventhgeneration.com

www.happyhippie.com

www.reuseablebags.com

www.reusethisbag.com

www.greenstudentu.com

HEALTH AND BEAUTY

BEAUTY SUPPLIES

www.drugstore.com

1-800-378-4786

drugstore.com sells everything you would need from a drugstore including makeup, skin care, hair care, contact lenses, medicines, personal care and much much more. There are instant coupons, clearance items, a 5% refund section and everyday they have new savings.
Shipping: Free on orders of $25
Return Policy: Within 30 days – follow online instructions.
Payment Methods: Major credit cards, Bill Me Later, Google Checkout and PayPal.

www.beauty.com

1-800-699-0015

A partner site with www.drugstore.com - two stores, one shopping bag. Dealing with skin care, makeup, fragrances, bath, body and hair care. Well-know brands include Philosophy, Frederic Fekkai, Fresh, Nars and many more.

www.buymebeauty.com

1-954-975-2400

Discounted makeup and beauty products from the world's most famous manufacturers including Estee Lauder, Lancome, Revlon, L'Oreal, Prescriptives, Almay and more.

Shipping: Free on order over $35
Return Policy: Contact customer service within 30 days to get details
Payment: Major credit cards

CONTACT LENSES

www.discountcontactlenses.com
1-800-822-9864

Major brands of contact lenses at lowest prices.

Shipping: Free on orders over $89 or choose at checkout.
Return Policy: No returns.
Payment: Major credit cards and Bill Me Later

Similar sites:

www.lensmart.com
1-800-693-8246

Shipping: Free
Payment Options: Major credit cards and Bill Me Later
Return Policy: If product unsatisfactory return within 30 days.

www.1800contacts.com
1-800-266-8228

Shipping: Free on orders over $80 or choose at checkout
Returns: No returns
Payment: Major credit cards, Bill Me Later

www.justlenses.com

1-800-516-5367

Shipping: Choose at checkout
Return Policy: Only if incorrect order
Payment: Major credit cards

www.shipmycontacts.com

1-800-975-7305

Shipping: Free on orders over $79 or choose at checkout
Return Options: Unopened items only within 30 days of delivery. Call customer service for RMA#
Payment Options: Major credit cards

HOMEOPATHY

www.herbalremedies.com

1-866-467-6444

Choose by brand, ailment, mineral, vitamin, herbal supplement or health supplement and a list of what you need comes up.

Shipping: Choose at checkout
Return Policy: Call or email customer service within 30 days for a RMA#.
Payment Options: Major credit cards, PayPal, Western Union

Similar website:

www.swansonvitamins.com

1-800-824-4491

Shipping: Flat rate $4.99 or choose at checkout
Return Policy: 100% guarantee on products returned within 12 months
Payment Options: Major credit cards

PERFUMES AND FRAGRANCES

www.perfume.com

1-800-645-9251

Find 100% genuine designer brands of perfume discounted at up to 80% off retail prices. Women's and men's fragrances as well as skincare and hair care products.

Shipping: Free on orders over $59
Return Policy: Call customer service for RMA# within 30 days of order. Must be in original packaging. 20% restocking fee.
Payment: Major credit cards.

www.fragrancenet.com

1-800-727-3867

fragrancenet.com sells 100% genuine designer brands of perfume including Calvin Klein, D&G, Versace, Fendi, Bulgari, Hermes and more at up to 60% off retail price. They also sell hair care and skin care products and candles at discount prices.

Shipping: Free on orders over $70
Returns: 30-day money back guarantee
Payment: Major credit cards, Bill Me Later, PayPal.

www.scentiments.com

1-800-685-7321

Many genuine designer scents for men and women including Abercrombie & Fitch, Armani, Beckham, Cartier, Chanel and more. First time users of the website get $20 off your first purchase of $50 or more.

Shipping: Free on orders over $75
Return Policy: 30 days in original condition.
Payment: Major credit cards, PayPal and Google Check-out

www.bigdiscountfragrances.com

1-866-948-4723

Authentic designer products at up to 90% off recommended retail price. Perfumes for women and colognes for men.

Shipping: Choose at checkout
Return Policy: Contact customer service within 30 days for RMA#. Must be in original unopened condition.
Payment Options: Major credit cards.

PRESCRIPTIONS ONLINE

The following sites are for prescriptions to be sent directly to you at home.

www.cvs.com

1-888-607-4287

Save up to 30% on all your prescriptions and call in for refills, then have them sent to your home.

Shipping: Free standard shipping or choose at checkout.
Return Policy: No returns on prescriptions ordered
Payment Options: Major credit cards

Similar sites:

www.drugstore.com

1-800-378-4786

Shipping: $2.99 flat rate
Return Policy: No returns on prescriptions
Payment Options: Major credit cards, PayPal, Google Checkout and Bill Me Later.

www.pharmnet.com

1-877-697-9638

Shipping: Standard shipping free on prescriptions or choose at checkout.
Return Policy: No returns on prescriptions
Payment Options: Major credit cards

VITAMINS

www.puritan.com

1-800-645-1030

Reliable company established 40 years ago. Vitamins, weight management products and herbal supplements. Many deals including some buy one get one free.

Shipping: Choose at checkout.
Return Policy: If not completely satisfied return within 365 days for refund.
Payment Options: Major credit cards

www.vitaminworld.com

1-866-667-8977

Sports nutrition, vitamins, diet products and aromatherapy all at 20%-50% off throughout the site.

Shipping: Flat rate $1.95 on any order or choose at checkout
Return Policy: If not satisfied return for refund.
Payment Options: Major credit cards

Similar sites:

www.911healthshop.com
1-800-764-9112

Shipping: Free on orders over $75 or choose at checkout.
Return Policy: Contact customer service within 30 days for RMA#. Some exceptions.
Payment Options: Major credit cards.

www.evitamins.com
1-888-222-6056

Shipping: Choose at checkout
Return Policy: Contact customer service for RMA#
Payment Options: Major credit cards.

HOBBIES

ART AND CRAFT

www.misterart.com

1-800-721-3015

One of the largest online discount art and craft supply stores. They offer all types of art and craft supplies, educational books and videos and kid's art supplies at up to 70% off regular retail prices. Misterart also has a V.I.P. club with an annual fee of $25 for even bigger discounts.

Shipping: Free on orders over $200 or choose at checkout.
Return Policy: Call customer service for RMA# within 30 days of order. Restocking fee applies.
Payment Options: Major credit cards, PayPal and money orders

www.Rexart.com

1-800-739-2782

Art and craft suppliers who offer 20-80% discount on weekly deals on all types of supplies including easels, finishes, paint, screen-printing, brushes, calligraphy and much more.

Shipping: Free on orders over $100 or choose at checkout
Return Policy: Call customer service within 30 days for RMA#. Some exclusions.
Payment Options: Major credit cards, PayPal and money orders

www.joann.com

1-888-739-4120

Shipping: Choose at checkout
Return Policy: Return in original package within 30 days if not satisfied. Return form in order.
Payment Options: Major credit cards

CAMPING EQUIPMENT

www.backcountryoutlet.com

1-800-409-4502

Everything for camping – outdoor clothes for men, women and kids, tents, sleeping bags, backpacks, camping furniture, cookware, car racks, lighting and much more.

Shipping: Free on orders over $50 or choose at checkout
Return Policy: Go online for RMA# to return item in original unused condition.
Payment Options: Major credit cards

Similar site:

www.campmor.com

1-800-525-4784

Shipping: Choose at checkout
Return Policy: Return slip on back of original invoice
Payment Options: Major credit cards

DANCEWEAR

www.allaboutdance.com

1-800-775-0578

allaboutdance.com always has up to 35% off retail prices for all types of dancewear, shoes, tights, undergarments and performance ensembles for all types of dance from ballet to ballroom to hip hop.
Items for girls, boys, men and women.

Shipping: Choose at checkout
Return Policy: Within 30 days of receipt. Must use RMA# which is sent with order. Some items excluded.
Payment Options: Major credit cards and PayPal

EDUCATION ONLINE

LANGUAGES

Go to any of these sites and learn a language at your own pace at home online.

www.mangolanguages.com

www.livemocha.com

www.babbel.com

www.elanguageschool.net

www.babelnation.com

ONLINE DEGREES

The following sites allow you to gain a degree online at your own pace.

www.onlinedegrees.com

www.homestudy.com

www.earnmydegree.com

www.degree.com

www.yourdegreesonline.com

SPORTS

FISHING TACKLE

www.landbigfish.com

1-877-347-4718

Over 70,000 online items for the avid fisherman – rods, reels, bait, clothes, traps and much more.

Shipping: Choose at checkout
Return Policy: If not satisfied contact customer service within 30 days for RMA#
Payment: MasterCard and Visa

KNITTING

www.knittingwarehouse.com

1-831-728-2584

Discount knitting and crochet supplies like yarn, needles, patterns, thread and all accessories you will need.

Shipping: Choose at checkout.
Return Policy: Call customer service for RMA# within 30 days of purchase.
Payment: Major credit cards

Similar sites:

www.bargainyarns.com

1-888-996-9278

Shipping: Choose at checkout
Return Policy: Contact customer service within 30 days for RMA#
No returns on books, patterns or needles.
Payment Options: Major credit cards

www.cheapknittingpatterns.com

1-920-954-1240

Website with hundreds of knitting epatterns available to download immediately.

SCRAPBOOKING

www.scrapbooksupercenter.com
1-800-659-4918

Deals on everything for the scrapbook fan from albums to memory kits to punches and stickers.

Shipping: Choose at checkout.
Return Policy: Call customer service for RMA# within 30 days of order. Special orders are non-refundable. Items over $100 are subject to 20% restocking fee.
Payment: Major credit cards

Similar site:

www.twopeasinabucket.com
1-888-896-7327

Shipping: Choose at checkout
Return Policy: No returns unless error in order
Payment: Major credit cards and PayPal

SEWING

www.sewingintheusa.com
1-888-872-7397

Sewing machines, embroidery machines, quilt shop, software and hardware, cases, covers, irons, presses, thread and much more.

Shipping: Choose at checkout.
Return Policy: Call customer service for RMA# within 30 days of order. Some items non-refundable. 15% restocking fee applies.
Payment: Major credit cards and PayPal

www.sewtrue.com
1-800-739-8783

Loads of patterns. Pay and download for immediate use. Also sells sewing machines, irons and accessories.

Shipping: Choose at checkout
Return Policy: Contact customer service within 30 days for RMA#
Payment Options: Major credit cards and PayPal

STAMP COLLECTING

www.stampcenter.com

1-410-757-5800

Premier stamp collecting dealer online.

Shipping: Choose at checkout.
Return Policy: Call customer service for RMA# within 15 days of order.
Payment: Major credit cards and PayPal

Similar site:

www.mdstamp.com

1-800-426-5723

Shipping: Choose at checkout
Return Policy: Call customer service within 30 days for RMA#. 10% restocking fee applies.
Payment: Visa and MasterCard

TOOLS

www.ToolsSoldHere.com

1-800-348-3841

Brand new site that I have previewed and opens soon. It has every tool for every job you might need from tightening a screw to major home improvements.

Shipping: Choose at checkout
Return Policy: Contact customer service within 30 days for RMA#
Payment Options: Major credit cards

www.themanstoreonline.com

1-866-630-9331

Themanstoreonline.com has tools for every household job from screws to ladders and for the bigger jobs.

Shipping: Choose at checkout
Return Policy: Contact customer service for RMA#. 25% restocking fee applies
Payment Options: Major credit cards.

Similar site:

www.thecontractorsexpress.com

1-616-534-1733

Shipping: Choose at checkout
Return Policy: Contact customer service within 30 days for
RMA#. 20% restocking fee applies.
Payment Options: Major credit cards

HOMES

KITCHEN APPLIANCES

www.kitchendirect.com

1-800-375-3128

Great savings on ranges, washers, dryers, ovens, cook tops, counters, faucets, sinks, dishwashers and more. Helps the customer find the product they need on budget and on time.

Shipping: Choose at checkout
Return Policy: Log onto account online to return. 20% restocking fee applies.
Payment Options: Major credit cards, Bill Me Later, PayPal, eBillMe, Google Checkout.

www.ajmadison.com

1-800-570-3355

This company deals in appliances for kitchen and laundry in sizes to fit in apartments.

Shipping: Choose at checkout
Return Policy: Call customer service for RMA#.
Payment Options: Major credit cards, Bill Me Later, PayPal.

Similar Sites:

HOMES

www.homedepot.com

www.lowes.com

www.searshomepro.com

HOME ACCESSORIES

www.egiftndecor.com
1-516-850-8369

This site offers 30-60% discount off home décor accessories for the entire home inside and outside.

Shipping: Choose at checkout
Return Policy: Within 30 days in original condition.
Payment: Major credit cards and PayPal

www.homedecorators.com
1-877-537-8539

Great discounted accessories for the home. They also have furniture and window treatments.

Shipping: Choose at checkout
Return Policy: Within 45 days of order go online and download return slip.
Payment: Major credit cards

Similar site:

www.onlinediscountmart.com

1-800-763-4177

Shipping: Choose at checkout.
Return Policy: Within 30 days of order. Restocking fee of 20% may apply.
Payment: Major credit cards or PayPal

CLOCKS

www.clockstyle.com

1-800-860-8992

clockstyle.com has all types of discount clocks including wall mounted, anniversary, outdoor, alarm, tabletop, desktop, cuckoo, floor and grandfather.

Shipping: Free shipping on many items given at checkout.
Return Policy: Contact customer service by phone or email for return process.
Payment Method: Major credit cards, Google Checkout, PayPal or Bill Me later.

MIRRORS

www.csnmirrors.com
1-800-584-0145

Mirrors for wall, floor, bathroom and vanity in all shapes and sizes.

Shipping: Free or choose at checkout
Return Policy: Within 30 days. Call customer service for RMA#.
Payment Options: Major credit cards, PayPal, Google Checkout

Similar site:

www.moremirrors.com
1-866-468-7320

Shipping: Choose at checkout
Return Policy: Within 60 days. Call customer service for RMA#.
Payment: Major credit cards

BED AND BATH

www.comfortchannel.com

1-800-303-7574

Bed and bath products that are hugely discounted, clearance section and some return items.

Shipping: Choose at checkout
Return Policy: Full refund on unopened items less shipping within 30 days of ordering. Restocking fee may apply, contact customer service for details.
Payment: Major credit cards and PayPal

www.bedbathstore.com

1-866-640-2400

Bedding, bath towels and accessories, including some organic products. Even bigger discounts for orders over $50 and $100.

Shipping: Free shipping promotion at times or choose at checkout.
Return Policy: Within 10 days if defective. Contact customer service.
Payment: Major credit cards and PayPal

www.designerlinensoutlet.com
1-866-725-3356

Many well-known designer bed and bath linens and weekly deals on already heavily discounted items.

Shipping: Flat rate.
Return Policy: Within 30 days of order. Pre-paid return address label is enclosed in order. Refund back to card less postage.
Payment: Major Credit Cards

Similar site:

www.annaslinens.com
1-866-266-2728

Shipping: Choose at checkout
Return Policy: Within 30 days, return information in package.
Payment Options: Major credit cards

CANDLES

www.generalwax.com

1-800-929-7867

generalwax.com designs and makes various candle collections in their own warehouse since 1949, including soy and beeswax. Great selection for every occasion and accessories like holders and hurricanes.

Shipping: Standard UPS or Fedex
Return Policy: Within 30 days of order. Call customer service for RMA# and fill in enclosed return label. Refund less shipping cost.
Payment: Major credit cards.

www.mellowcandles.com

1-864-363-0545

Specializes in novelty bakery, dessert, ice cream and cocktail candles which make wonderful gifts. Plus soy and gel candles.

Shipping: Choose at checkout
Returns: Within 20 days of order – unwrapped and unused. Credit to card minus 30% restocking charge and shipping costs.
Payment: Major credit cards and PayPal

www.discountcandleshop.com
1-866-205-6376

discountcandleshop.com features candle kits, holiday themed candles, floating, wedding and candle making supplies.

Shipping: Free shipping over $50
Returns: In original packaging. Restocking fee of 15% plus shipping costs.
Payment: Major credit cards, PayPal and Money Order

CARPETS, RUGS AND FLOOR COVERINGS

www.carpetwagon.com

1-877-273-2449

Carpetwagon.com supplies carpet, laminate and hardwood floors. Shop at home. A design expert will come with choices for floor covering, measure your floors and arrange an installation date.

www.fastfloors.com

1-800-764-1212

All types of flooring, bamboo, cork, wood, laminate, rubber, tile, stone and vinyl and all at wholesale or below.

Shipping: Some free or choose at checkout
Return Policy: Differs on products. Contact customer service within 30 days of receipt.
Payment Options: Major credit cards

www.esalerugs.com

1-866-647-3965

A large selection of Persian, oriental and modern rugs at hugely discounted prices.

Shipping: Free
Return Policy: 7 days from receipt of product. Call for RMA#.
Payment: Major credit cards or PayPal.

www.bestrugs.com

1-800-416-5508

Features a huge range of styles and colors of rugs.

Shipping: Free shipping
Returns: 14 days return policy from the day received. Call for RMA#.
Payment: Major credit cards, PayPal

www.efloors.com

1-888-775-7595

efloors.com deals with laminate, hardwood and vinyl flooring as well as area rugs.

Shipping: Free shipping and free underlay.
Return Policy: 14 days after receipt of product. Call for RMA#.
Payment: Major credit cards and PayPal.

COOKWARE

www.chefscorner.com

1-877-372-4235

Great website for everything for the kitchen and more. Cookware, bakeware, cutlery, coffee and tea, kitchen tools, small electrics, cookbooks, tableware and much more.

Shipping: Choose at checkout
Return Policy: Contact customer service within 30 days for RMA#. 50% restocking fee applies.
Payment Options: Major credit cards, PayPal and Bill Me Later

www.instawares.com

1-800-892-3622

instawares.com has all kinds of discount cookware and pots and pans from cast iron to steamers, woks, and roasters. Selling to restaurants as well as the public.

Shipping: Free on orders over $50 or choose at checkout.
Return Policy: Within 15 days of delivery, returns subject to 25% restocking fee and shipping charges. Go online for RMA#.
Payment Method: Major credit cards and PayPal

www.cooking.com

1-800-663-8810

Everything for your kitchen from pots, pans, knives, table-ware, and cutlery to barbeque items and small appliances.

Shipping: Flat rate with code on website or choose at checkout
Return Policy: Fill in return form online
Payment: Major credit cards

Similar sites:

www.paylesscookware.com

1-888-878-9989

Shipping: Choose at checkout
Return Policy: Contact customer service online for RMA# within 30 days of purchase.
Payment Options: Major credit cards and PayPal

www.cookware.com

1-888-478-4606

Shipping: Choose at checkout
Return Policy: Contact customer service within 30 days. 20% restocking fee applies.
Payment Options: Major credit cards and PayPal

www.cutleryandmore.com

via email

Huge variety of kitchen knives and tools plus cookware.

Shipping: Free on orders over $49 or choose at checkout
Return Policy: Return within 30 days with original invoice.
Payment Options: Major credit cards and PayPal

FLATWARE

www.oneina.com
1-888-263-7195

50% discount on top designs of modern, classic and decorative flatware and serving sets.

Shipping: Choose at checkout
Return Policy: Within 30 days. Return slip on reverse of original invoice.
Payment Options: Major credit cards

www.americandiscountflatware.com
1-877-544-8046

Wholesale prices for flatware and steak knives with a choice of 27 different patterns.

Shipping: Choose at checkout
Return Policy: Within 30 days. Call customer service for RMA#. 25% restocking fee applies.
Payment: Major credit cards

FIREPLACES

www.fireplacesnow.com

1-877-669-4669

Fireplaces and inserts, wood burning, vent-free, stoves, out-door, electric, gas logs, glass doors and accessories

Shipping: Free on orders over $50 or choose at checkout
Return Policy: Contact customer service within 30 days for RMA#. 20% restocking fee applies.
Payment Options: Major credit cards

www.electricfireplaces.com

1-800-555-0564

Fireplace inserts, stoves, log sets, outdoor electric fireplaces and barbeques, wall and corner mantels and wall mount electric fires.

Shipping: Free or choose at checkout
Return Policy: Must get RMA# from customer service within 48 hours of receiving your order. Return freight charges will not be refunded.
Payment Options: Major credit cards, PayPal and Google Checkout

www.mantelsdirect.com

1-888-493-8898

Made-to-measure fireplace mantels and shelves, as well as gas, electric and outdoor fireplaces.

Shipping: Sometimes free or choose at checkout
Return Policy: Contact customer service within 14 days only if in original packaging.
Payment Options: Major credit cards, PayPal and checks by phone.

FLOWERS

www.proflowers.com

1-800-580-2913

Send flowers or plants to yourself or family and friends – discounts vary daily. Flowers for all occasions.

Shipping: Choose at checkout
Return Policy: No returns
Payment Options: Major credit card

Similar sites:

www.bloomstoday.com

1-800-520-0573

Shipping: Standard $13.99 or choose at checkout
Return Policy: No returns
Payment Options: Major credit cards

www.onlineflowers.com

1-800-793-6766

Shipping: Flat rate $13.99 or choose at checkout
Return Policy: 100% satisfaction guaranteed
Payment Options: Major credit cards

FURNITURE

www.homeclick.com
1-800-643-9990

Great online retail store with absolutely everything for the home – appliances, tableware, fireplaces, furniture, lighting, hardware, home decor and outdoor items.

Shipping: Free on orders over $199 or choose at checkout
Return Policy: Contact customer service within 30 days for RMA#. 15% restocking applies.
Payment Options: Major credit cards, PayPal, Bill Me Later

www.everythingfurniture.com
1-877-209-7908

Furniture for every room in the house plus accessories. They also have a sale and close out section with bigger discounts.

Shipping: Choose at checkout
Return Policy: Contact customer service within 15 days for RMA#. Restocking fee of 15% applies.
Payment Options: Major credit card, PayPal and check by fax.

www.onewayfurniture.com
1-800-789-1995

onewayfurniture.com has furniture for every room in the house and outdoors including children and baby rooms.

Shipping: Free
Return Policy: Within 30 days – 15% restocking fee and shipping
Payment Options: Major credit cards and money orders.

Similar sites:

www.ifurn.com
1-877-683-9393

Shipping: Free on most items
Return Policy: Must get RMA# within 15 days. 20% restocking fee applies.
Payment Options: Major credit cards

www.roomstogo.com
1-800-709-5380

Shipping: 15% of purchase price
Return Policy: Within 30 days, charge for shipping
Payment Options: Major credit cards and money orders

www.bellacor.com

1-877-723-5522

Shipping: Free on orders over $75
Return Policy: No hassle return for refund less shipping cost
Payment Options: Major credit cards

www.readysethome.com

1-888-903-7495

Shipping: Free on orders over $500 or choose at checkout
Return Policy: Contact customer service within 10 days for
RMA#. 15% restocking fee applies.
Payment Options: Major credit cards

www.furnitureplaza.com

1-866-788-2202

Shipping: Free and no tax
Return Policy: Contact customer service within 14 days for
RMA#. 15% restocking fee applies.
Payment Options: Major credit cards

www.bedroomfurniture.com

1-800-311-4137

Shipping: Free
Return Policy: Contact customer service within 30 days for
RMA#.
Payment Options: Major credit cards and PayPal.

LIGHTING AND LAMPS

www.lampsplus.com

1-800-782-1967

The online version of the store with a vast selection of ceiling lights, lamps, wall lights, outdoor lights, ceiling fans and accessories.
They have a 120% price protection – if within 60 days of your purchase you find an identical item for less at a competitor they will match the price and refund 20% of price difference.

Shipping: Choose at checkout
Return Policy: Mandatory to get a RMA# from customer service within 60 days of purchase.
Payment: Major credit cards. Bill Me Later.

Similar sites:

www.lightingdirect.com

1-800-375-3410

Shipping: Free on orders of $49 or more or choose at checkout.
Return Policy: Get RMA# from customer service within 30 days.
Payment Options: Major credit cards, Bill Me Later, Google Checkout, PayPal and eBillMe

www.lampsusa.com
1-877-526-7247

Shipping: Free on orders over $99 or choose at checkout
Return Policy: Contact customer service within 14 days of purchase for RMA#. 25% restocking fee applies
Payment Options: Major credit cards

www.1stoplighting.com
1-866-203-5392

Shipping: Free on orders over $200 or choose at checkout.
Return Policy: Must get RMA# from customer service within 15 days of purchase. 25% restocking fee and freight charges apply.
Payment Options: Major credit cards.

www.lumens.com
1-877-445-4486

Shipping: Free on orders over $50 or choose at checkout
Return Policy: Contact customer service within 30 days for RMA#
Payment Options: Major credit cards, PayPal and Google Checkout

www.exteriorlightinguniverse.com

1-877-247-8990

Shipping: Free on orders over $49 or choose at checkout.
Return Policy: Contact customer service within 30 days of purchase. Some restocking fees apply.
Payment Options: Major credit cards, PayPal, eBillMe, Google Checkout.

www.1000bulbs.com

1-800-624-4488

Light bulbs of all shapes, sizes and colors.

Shipping: Choose at checkout
Return Policy: Go online within 30 days of purchase for mandatory RMA#. 35% restocking fee applies.
Payment Options: Major credit cards.

www.novalightingstore.com

1-800-860-1207

Shipping: Mostly free or choose at checkout
Return Policy: Contact customer service within 5 days for RMA#. Restocking fee of 25% applies
Payment Options: Major credit cards

MATTRESSES

www.1stopmattress.com
1-888-726-1233

1stopmattress.com has all types and sizes of mattresses at excellent prices 40-70% below retail prices, including well-know brand names.

They also sell bedroom furniture.

Shipping: Choose at checkout
Return Policy: No return on mattresses. Others items call customer service for a RMA#.
Payment Options: Major credit cards

Similar sites:

www.moremattresses.com
1-866-740-9830

Shipping: Choose at checkout
Return Policy: Within 30 days. Call customer service for details
Payment Options: Major credit cards, Bill Me Later, eBillMe, PayPal, Google Checkout.

www.americasmattress.com

1-714-288-0530

Shipping: Choose at checkout
Return Policy: No returns on mattresses.   Call customer service for RMA# for other items
Payment Options: Major credit cards

www.mydreammattress.com

1-800-248-1987

Shipping: Choose at checkout
Return Policy: No returns
Payment Options: Major credit cards and PayPal

OUTDOOR FURNITURE

www.patiofurnitureusa.com

1-800-351-5699

A leading source for all types of patio furniture including wood, wicker, wrought iron and aluminum, from loungers to dining tables.
Plus fire pits, gazebos, lighting accessories.

Shipping: Choose checkout
Return Policy: No hassle returns. Contact customer service within 30 days for a RMA#
Payment Options: Major credit cards, PayPal, Bill Me Later, Google Checkout.

www.outdoordecor.com

1-800-422-1525

Large online retailer with competitive prices on everything for the garden including fountains, greenhouses, benches, heating, lighting, furniture.

Shipping: Choose at checkout.
Return Policy: Contact customer service within 30 days for RMA#.
Payment Options: Major credit cards

Similar site:

www.outdoorgardenfurniture.com

1-800-969-6876

Shipping: Free on orders over $99 or choose at checkout
Return Policy: No returns unless delivered damaged
Payment Options: Major credit cards and PayPal

BARBEQUES

www.outdoorlivingshowroom.com

1-800-353-6907

outdoorlivingshowroom.com sells many types and makes of barbeques and grills as well as accessories, smokers, cookware plus outdoor furniture.

Shipping: Free on orders over $49
Returns Policy: 30 day no hassle returns as new. Some items are liable to restocking fee. Call customer service for RMA#.
Payment: Major credit cards, PayPal, eBillMe and Google Checkout.

Similar site:

www.grillsdirect.com

1-800-590-3829

Shipping: Choose at checkout
Return Options: Satisfaction guaranteed. Contact customer service.
Restocking fee applies.
Payment Options: Major credit cards, Bill Me Later, PayPal and Google Checkout.

GARDEN PLANTS

www.directgardening.com

1-309-662-7943

Offers all kinds of seeds, bulbs, shrubs, vegetables, vines, roses, pond supplies, fertilizer, bird feeders and much more.

Shipping: Choose at checkout
Return Policy: If any items do not live for a year they will re-place free of charge. Other items must be returned within 14 days with original invoice.
Payment Options: Visa and MasterCard

www.greatgardenplants.com

1-877-447-4769

Greatly discounted rose, perennials, trees, shrubs, hedge plants and many more options. Plus containers, soil and accessories.

Shipping: Choose at checkout
Return Policy: If not satisfied call customer service immedi-ately for RMA#.
Payment: Major credit cards

POOL SUPPLIES

www.aquasuperstore.com
1-866-910-2782

Everything you could possible want for your pool including chemicals, auto cleaners, covers, heaters, filters, pumps and loads more all at discounted prices.

Shipping: Choose at checkout
Return Policy: Must be within 30 days of purchase, go online to fill out RMA form
Payment Options: Major credit cards, PayPal

Similar sites:

www.americasbestpoolsupply.com
1-888-284-6007

Shipping: Choose at checkout
Return Policy: Must get RMA# from customer service within 30 days of purchase. 15% restocking fee applies
Payment Options: Major credit cards

www.cheappoolproducts.com
1-800-990-8595

Shipping: Free on orders over $50 or choose at checkout
Return Policy: Go online for RMA form within 30 days of purchase
Payment Options: MasterCard and Visa

WINDOW TREATMENTS

BLINDS

www.blindschalet.com

1-877-702-5463

Any type of blinds and shades you could want including wood, faux wood, cellular, aluminum, bamboo, fabric, rollers and more with lifetime warranty.

Shipping: Free or choose at checkout.
Return Policy: Call customer service within 30 days for RMA# is defective or damaged.
Payment Options: Major credit cards, Bill Me later, PayPal.

www.selectblinds.com

1-877-705-7418

All types of blinds – wood, faux wood, vertical, and mini plus window shades. Easy to use details of how to measure and install. Get free swatch before you order.

Shipping: Free on orders under 90 inches or choose at checkout.
Return Policy: Must contact customer service.
Payment Options: Major credit cards, PayPal and Bill Me Later

Similar sites:

www.justblinds.com
1-800-959-9939

Shipping: Free on orders under 93 inches, or choose at checkout.
Return Policy: Must contact customer service within 30 days.
Payment Options: Major credit cards and Bill Me Later

www.blindsgalore.com
1-877-702-5463

Shipping: Free or choose at checkout
Return Policy: Contact customer service for RMA# if defective or damaged.
Payment Options: Major credit cards, Bill Me later

DRAPES

www.factorybargaindrapes.com

1-866-713-7273

This site sells drapes at 50-80% off retail store prices. Search by style, color, fabric and size. Measuring details on site. Sample and swatches available.

Shipping: Choose at checkout
Return Policy: All sales final
Payment Options: Major credit card, PayPal.

Similar site:

www.halfpricedrapes.com

1-866-413-7273

Shipping: Choose at checkout
Return Policy: Varies, contact customer service
Payment Options: Major credit cards

KIDS

CLOTHES

www.kidsurplus.com

1-866-543-3325

kidsurplus.com has kids clothes from newborns to 16 years old for boys and girls. Favorite names at unbeatable discount prices.

Shipping: Free on orders over $79
Return Policy: Within 30 days, credit less shipping charges
Payment Options: Major credit cards, PayPal, wire transfer or money order.

Similar sites:

www.webclothes.com

1-888-575-9303

Shipping: Choose at checkout
Return Policy: Within 30 days of purchase for refund excluding shipping charges. Return label included in order.
Payment Options: Major credit cards

www.bargainchildrenclothing.com

via email

Shipping: Choose at checkout
Return Policy: Within 30 days. RMA# is included in order, must send it with return.
Payment Option: Major credit cards.

KIDS

www.kidswearhouse.net
1-585-643-5437

Shipping: Flat rate $5.99 or choose at checkout
Return Policy: Within 21 days of receipt. Must get RMA#
from customer service – store credit only
Payment Options: Major credit cards and PayPal

SHOES

www.zappos.com

1-800-927-7671

Shipping: Free standard or choose at checkout
Return Policy: Up to 365 days of purchase date in original condition.
Payment Options: Major credit cards, Bill Me Later and PayPal

www.shoemall.com

1-800-704-5478

Shipping: Free standard or choose at checkout
Return Policy: Return slip in order. Free return shipping.
Payment: Major credit cards, Bill Me Later

KIDS LEARNING AND GAMES

Below are some of the best free websites for kids of all ages. There are hundreds of games, puzzles, activities, both online and printable. Plus new educational and playful activities added regularly.

www.bigfishgames.com

www.more4kids.info

www.thekidzpage.com

www.neopets.com

www.zeeks.com

www.coloringpage.org

www.headbonezone.com

www.pawisland.com

www.kids.com

www.animaland.com

www.funschool.com

www.yucky.com

www.iknowthat.com

www.kidsclick.org

www.funbrain.com

www.uptoten.com

www.funology.com

www.kbears.com

www.learn4good.com

www.kindersite.com

www.kidsknowit.com

www.kidsnumbers.com

www.freestuff4kids.com

www.craynola.com

USEFUL SITES

KIDS RESEARCH SITES

Research sites for kids:

www.awesomelibrary.com

www.askkids.com

www.howstuffworks.com

www.dibdabdoo.com

www.cybersleuth.com

www.yahookids.com

www.kidsclick.com

www.kidskonnect.com

www.ajkids.com

www.yahooligans.com

www.factmonster.com

www.kids.gov

www.family-source.com

TOYS

www.stickergiant.com

1-866-774-7900

Hundreds of stickers including some free. Also upload your artwork and print your own.

Shipping: Free or $5 discount, choose at checkout
Return Policy: If not satisfied they will give a full refund.
Payment Options. Major credit cards

www.allaboardtoys.com

1-866-641-8697

Huge range of discounted toys, bedding and party supplies.

Shipping: Choose at checkout
Return Policy: Go online within 30 days of purchase for return form.
Payment Options: Major credit cards, PayPal and Google Checkout.

www.toysrus.com
via email

A top-rated website from a long time retail store. Many deals and sales on the hottest toys, games and video games for kids of all ages.

Shipping: Free when spending over $25 or based on weight.
Return Policy: Within 30 days. Unopened packaging for videos and games. Original condition. Return slip in package, postage deducted from refund.
Payment: Major credit cards, ToysRUs Visa, or gift card.

www.joissu.com
1-800-233-1681

Wholesale toys, novelties and gifts. General public can purchase with a minimum order of $50.

Shipping: Standard
Returns: All sales final. No returns unless damaged on arrival.
Payment: Major credit cards.

www.backtobasictoys.com

1-800-356-5360

Discounted classic, quality toys and playthings for learning.

Shipping: Choose at checkout
Return Policy: 100% satisfaction guaranteed within 60 days of purchase. Return slip in order.
Payment Options: Major credit cards

www.discountschoolsupplies.com

1-800-627-2829

Products for early learners including arts and crafts, school supplies, educational toys and much more.

Shipping: Free on orders over $79 or choose at checkout
Return Policy: Contact customer service.
Payment Options: Major credit cards and PayPal

MENS

CLOTHES

www.menswearhouse.com
1-800-776-7848

Great deals all the time, even buy one suit get another free. Every type of men's clothing including sports coats, suits, outwear and sportswear for all sizes including big and tall. They also have tuxedo rentals.

Shipping: Free ground shipping on orders over $100 or choose at checkout.
Return Policy: Return within 90 days of order in unused condition. Return slip in original order.
Payment Options: Major credit cards

www.sierratradingpost.com
1-800-713-4534

30% to 70% off all types of men's apparel from underwear to casual and business suits, plus shoes, boots and accessories. Brand names include Ralph Lauren and Bill Blass. 20% off your first order.

Shipping: Some free, choose at checkout
Return Policy: Return form enclosed in order on back of invoice.
Payment Options: Major credit cards, PayPal, Google Checkout

MENS

www.menswear-discounts.com
1-866-761-1500

Discount designer menswear. Ralph Lauren, tuxedos, suits, outerwear, sports coats, slacks and a big and tall section.

Shipping: Choose at checkout
Return Policy: 15 day unconditional money back guarantee. Email customer service for RMA#,
Payment Options: Major credit cards and money order

www.mensredtag.com
1-866-942-4243

Shipping: Choose at checkout
Return Policy: Contact customer service within 30 days for RMA#
Payment Options: Major credit cards

BIG AND TALL

www.onestopplus.com

1-800-400-4481

Well-known brands for men's big and tall, Clothes from casual to dress, active wear and outerwear. Sizes XL-10XL and shoes sizes to 17EEEEE.

Shipping: Choose at checkout
Return Policy: Contact customer service within 90 days.
Payment Options: Major credit cards

Similar sites:

www.casualmale.com

1-800-767-0319

Shipping: Choose at checkout
Return Policy: Online for RMA#
Payment Options: Major credit cards

www.bigmansland.com

1-866-363-5100

Shipping: Choose at checkout
Return Policy: Contact customer service within 30 days for RMA#
Payment Options: Major credit cards

www.shoesxl.com
1-800-690-7377

Hard to find men's shoes and boots in sizes 12M and 10W on up.

Shipping: Choose at checkout
Return Policy: Go online for return form
Payment Options: Major credit cards

FORMAL WEAR

www.cheaptux.com
1-888-245-0148

Full tuxedo packages, trousers, shirts, bowties, vests, jackets, shoes and accessories.

Shipping: Free
Return Policy: Contact customer service within 30 days for RMA#. 20% restocking fee applies
Payment Options: Major credit cards, PayPal, money orders and checks.

Similar sites:

www.finetuxedos.com
1-888-577-2760

Shipping: Choose at checkout
Return Policy: Unused only within 30 days of purchase contact customer service for RMA#
Payment Options: Major credit cards

www.tuxedoonline.com
1-888-968-4889

Shipping: Choose at checkout
Return Policy: Request RMA for online within 30 days of purchase. 25% restocking fee applies.
Payment Options: Major credit cards, PayPal, Google Checkout.

SHAVING SUPPLIES

www.amazingshaving.com
1-800-962-5003

Men's shaving products including shaving kits, aftershave, shaving mugs, brushes and soap, straight edge and safety razors, moustache wax and more.

Shipping: Choose at checkout
Return Policy: Contact customer service within 30 days for RMA#. Unopened items only.
Payment Options: Major credit cards and PayPal

www.classicshaving.com
1-760-288-4178

Old school shaving supplies with a wide variety of razors, brushes, creams, mugs and bowls, grooming sets and more.

Shipping: Choose at checkout
Return Policy: Contact customer service within 30 days for RMA#. Unused items only.
Payment Options: Major credit cards, PayPal and money orders

www.razordirect.com
via email

Every kind of razor, blades and cartridges you could want at discount prices.

Shipping: Choose at checkout
Return Policy: Satisfaction guaranteed
Payment Options: Major credit cards and PayPal

SHOES AND BOOTS

www.shoebuy.com

1-800-200-8414

Find weekly savings on already discounted prices on over 800 brands, many well-known, of shoes and boots from dress to athletic. Also for women and kids.

Shipping: Free ground or choose at checkout. Free return shipping.
Return Policy: Within 60 days use return UPS label in order.
Payment Options: Major credit cards, PayPal, Bill Me Later, Google Checkout, eBillMe, Western Union.

www.copshoes.com

1-866-280-0400

Not just for law enforcement! This family-owned company features a huge assortment of heavy duty boots and shoes for work and all outdoor activities. Brands include Timber-land, Dickies and Oakley.

Shipping: Choose at checkout
Return Policy: Contact customer service for RMA#. $10 restocking fee applies
Payment Options: Major credit cards and PayPal
Similar sites:

www.zappos.com

1-800-927-7671

Shipping: Choose at checkout
Return Policy: Up to 365 days from purchase if returned in same condition. Free return shipping.
Payment Options: Major credit cards, Bill Me Later and PayPal

www.onlyslippers.com

1-866-370-1120

Shipping: Choose at checkout
Return Policy: Within 30 days, restocking fee applies.
Payment Options: Major credit cards, Bill Me Later and PayPal

www.onlineshoes.com

1-800-786-3141

Shipping: Choose at checkout
Return Policy: Within 90 days. Go online for return label
Payment Options: Major credit cards

www.discountboots.com

1-877-609-6655

Shipping: Free
Return Policy: Unused items only.
Payment Options: Major credit cards and PayPal.

www.sportsmansguide.com

1-888-844-0667

Shipping: Choose at checkout
Return Policy: Return slip on back of invoice
Payment Options: Major credit cards

WIGS AND HAIRPIECES

www.wowwigs.com

1-866-969-9447

Thousands of wig styles, hairpieces and extensions for fun, fasion and costumes. Discount coupons for up to 30% off.

Shipping: Free on orders over $49.95 or choose at check-out
Return Policy: No returns
Payment Options: Major credit cards and PayPal

www.hairdirect.com

1-800-424-7436

Hairdirect.com has a hair replacement system custom fit for you to do at home, includes DVD to show how.

Shipping: Free
Return Policy: 100% money back guarantee
Payment Options: Major credit cards

OFFICE SUPPLIES

CUSTOMIZED PROMOTIONAL ITEMS

www.inkhead.com

1-800-554-0127

Website for all sorts of customized promotional items including apparel, bags, drinkware, journals, notebooks, pens, pencils and hundreds more. Upload your artwork and they will email a free virtual proof.

Shipping: Choose at checkout
Return Policy: No returns on personalized items. Other returns within 30 days and 10% restocking fee applies.
Payment Options: Major credit cards

www.discountpens.com

1-800-569-1980

Discountpens.com offer a wide variety of promotional pens for business, wedding favors or promotional giveaways. Choose from many colors and styles, then upload your logo or artwork and they do the rest. Also available: personalized mouse pads and mugs.

Shipping: Choose at checkout
Return Policy: No returns on custom work
Payment Options: Major credit cards

OFFICE FURNITURE

www.officefurniture.com

1-800-933-0053

Computer desks, office chairs, bookcases, tv stands, file cabinets and everything you need to furnish your office.

Shipping: Choose at checkout.
Return Policy: Office supplies within 30 days in original un-opened packaging. Contact customer service for RMA#, restocking fees and freight charges.
Payment Options: Major credit cards

Similar site:

www.officefurniture2go.com

1-800-460-0858

Shipping: Free
Return Policy: Contact customer service within one week of receipt for RMA#. Must be in original packaging.
Payment Options: Major credit cards

INK AND TONER

www.worldclassink.com

1-877-813-7201

Never waste time and gas shopping for ink and toner again! This amazing site features ink and toner for all printers and fax machines. Also labels, specialty paper and film.

Shipping: Free on all cartridge orders or choose at checkout
Return Policy: Unopened items must be returned within 90 days. 20% restocking fee applies.
Payment Options: Major credit cards and PayPal

Similar sites:

www.abcink.com

1-626-917-0668

Shipping: Free or choose at checkout for next day.
Return Policy: Click on site within 30 days for RMA#.
Payment Options: Major credit cards and PayPal

www.asapink.com

1-888-323-2727

Shipping: Free on all orders
Return Policy: Complete online RMA# request form and wait for email.
Payment Options: Major credit cards and PayPal

SUPPLIES

www.inkcloners.com
1-866-274-2821

Shipping: Free on order over $50 or choose and checkout
Return Policy: Online RMA# form and wait for return email
Payment Options: Major credit cards and PayPal

www.clickinks.com
1-800-706-4657

Shipping: Free on orders over $50 or choose at checkout
Return Policy: Click on support center for details.
Payment Options: Major credit cards, PayPal and Google Checkout

www.123inkjets.com
1-888-465-7765

Shipping: Free on orders over $55 or choose at checkout
Return Policy: Within 365 days for full refund unopened only
Payment Options: Major credit cards, PayPal and Google Checkout

www.toner.com

1-727-444-4444

Shipping: Choose at checkout
Return Policy: Contact customer service for RMA#
Payment Options: Major credit cards

OFFICE SUPPLIES

www.officedepot.com
1-800-463-3768

The online branch of this national office supply company has weekly deals on all things from office supplies to technology to furniture.

Shipping: Choose at checkout. Free on orders over $50
Return Policy: Office supplies within 30 days in original unopened packaging. Technology and furniture within 14 days of purchase. 15% restocking fee applies.
Payment Options: Major credit cards

www.officemax.com
1-800-283-7674

Shipping: Choose at checkout. Free shipping on orders over $50
Return Policy: If not satisfied return within 14 days in original package.
Payment Options: Major credit cards and Bill Me Later

www.shoplet.com
1-877-746-7001

Shipping: Choose at checkout. Free on orders over $45
Return Policy: Must go online for RMA#
Payment Options: Major credit cards, eBillMe and PayPal

www.officesupplygroup.com

1-800-346-0395

Shipping: Choose at checkout
Refund Policy: Within 30 days in original sealed package.
Contact customer service for RMA#
Payment Options: PayPal, major credit cards, Google
Checkout

www.office1000.com

via email

Shipping: Free on orders over $100 or choose at checkout
Return Policy: Contact customer service within 10 days for
RMA#.
25% restocking fee applies.
Payment: Major credit cards

STATIONERY

www.americanstationery.com

1-800-822-2577

American Stationery manufactures their own products so are able to set good prices. Personalized stationery and address labels, greeting cards for all occasions, invitations. Also business stationery and pens and an eco-friendly section.

Shipping: Choose at checkout
Return Policy: Contact customer service
Payment Options: Major credit cards

RUBBER STAMPS

www.discountrubberstamps.com

1-800-348-1689

Up to 70% off retail prices on many styles of stamps for home or business. Personalized stamps available.

Shipping: Choose at checkout
Return Policy: No returns
Payment Options: Major credit cards

Similar site:

www.rubberstampchamp.com

1-800-469-7826

Shipping: Free on orders over $100 or choose at checkout
Return Policy: No returns unless manufacturers error.
Payment Options: Major credit cards and PayPal

PET SUPPLIES

FOOD AND SUPPLIES

www.petfooddirect.com

1-800-865-1333

Food for all pets – dogs, cats, birds, fish, horses, reptiles and other small pets. Top brand names including natural and organic products. Books, pet travel center, weight management, senior care, litter care and much more. Some deals at 70% discount, and they have a rewards program.
Shipping: Some items free standard or choose at checkout
Return Policy: If not 100% satisfied contact customer service for RMA#
Payment Options: Major credit cards.

Similar sites:

www.pawsuppetsupply.com

1-877-604-7877

Shipping: Free on orders over $75 or choose at checkout
Return Policy: 365 day return policy
Payment Options: MasterCard, Visa and PayPal

www.petwholesaler.com

1-877-321-5050

Shipping: Choose at checkout
Return Policy: Varies on items. Call customer service
Payment Options: Major credit cards

www.sitstay.com
1-800-748-7829

Shipping: Choose at checkout
Return Policy: Returns accepted unused within 60 days of receipt. Return label in order
Payment Options: Major credit cards

www.pet-dog-cat-supply-store.com
1-866-331-1920

Shipping: Choose at checkout
Return Policy: Within 30 days get RMA# - 15% restocking fee applies
Payment Options: Major credit cards

PET MEDICATION

www.1800petmeds.com

1-800-738-6337

Largest online pet pharmacy for prescription and non-pre-scription medication. They will match the price of FDA/EPA approved product if you find an item cheaper elsewhere.

Shipping: Free on orders over $39 or choose at checkout
Return Policy: Online return label.
Payment Options: Major credit cards

SPORTS

BASEBALL

www.baseballsavings.com

1-866-923-5050

Everything for baseball – balls, bats, gloves, pads, protective gear bags, helmets, shoes, apparel, field equipment and accessories.

Shipping: Choose at checkout
Return Policy: Contact customer service for RMA# within 30 days of purchase.
Payment Options: Major credit cards

Similar site:

www.baseballrampage.com

1-800-758-8778

Shipping: Free on orders over $99 or choose at checkout.
Return Policy: Contact customer service within 30 days of purchase for RMA#.
Payment Options: Major credit cards, PayPal and Bill Me Later

BASKETBALL

www.hitrunscore.com

1-800-660-8815

Everything for hoops – basketballs, backboards, portable equipment, poles, rims, padding, bags, training equipment, apparel and accessories.

Shipping: Choose at checkout
Return Policy: Contact customer service for RMA# within 30 days of purchase. 20% restocking fee applies
Payment Options: Major credit cards

FOOTBALL

www.footballamerica.com

1-866-816-9835

Everything for football – uniforms, shoulder pads, helmets, facemasks, footwear and accessories.

Shipping: Choose at checkout
Return Policy: 30 days in original condition – 25% restocking fee applies
Payment Options: Major credit cards

GOLF

www.global.com

1-866-843-0262

Huge discounts on many brands of golf clubs, shoes, bags, balls, apparel and accessories including a clearance section with even bigger discounts. Everything golf for men and women, including pre-owned items.

Shipping: Choose at checkout
Return Policy: Pre-owned items within 14 days and new items within 30 days in original condition. Call customer service for RMA# for all returns.
Payment Options: Major credit cards, PayPal and Google Checkout

www.3balls.com

1-508-8212-3900

Amazing deals on everything golf – balls, shoes, equipment, apparel and accessories.

Shipping: Free on orders over $100 or choose at checkout.
Return Policy: Contact customer service for RMA#
Payment Options: Major credit cards and PayPal

Similar sites:

www.golfshoesonly.com

1-866-272-0099

Shipping: Choose at checkout
Return Policy: Call customer service within 30 days for RMA#
Payment Options: Major credit cards.

www.golfcow.com

1-877-317-4653

Shipping: Choose at checkout
Return Policy: Return within 30 days. 20% restocking fee applies.
Payment Options: Major credit cards.

www.golfballs.com

1-800-372-2557

Shipping: Choose at checkout
Return Policy: Within 30 days
Payment Options: Major credit cards

GYM EQUIPMENT

www.bigfitness.com

1-800-383-2008

One of the largest dealers in fitness equipment. Products include home gyms, ellipticals, treadmills, bikes, and exercise balls, weight lifting gear and all accessories. They also offer 110% lowest price guarantee.

Shipping: Choose at checkout
Return Policy: Contact customer service within 30 days for RMA#.
Payment Options: Major credit cards, PayPal and Money Order

Similar sites:

www.smoothfitness.com

1-888-211-1611

Shipping: Some free or choose at checkout
Return Policy: Contact customer service within 30 days to obtain RMA#.
Payment Options: Major credit cards, PayPal and Google Checkout

www.workoutwarehouse.com

1-888-308-0627

Shipping: Some free or choose at checkout
Return Policy: Contact customer service within 30 days for
RMA#. 10% restocking fee applies.
Payment Options: Major credit cards

www.net2fitness.com

1-727-943-8195

Shipping: Choose at checkout
Return Policy: Contact customer service within 10 days for
RMA# 20% restocking fee applies
Payment Options: Major credit cards and PayPal

HOCKEY

www.discounthockey.com

1-800-650-4834

Everything for hockey – skates, gloves, pads, guards, sticks, bags, helmets and accessories.

Shipping: Free on orders over $170 or choose at checkout
Return Policy: Online return RMA# form within 30 days of purchase.
Payment Options: Major credit cards

SPORTS MEMORABILIA

www.prosportsmemorabilia.com

1-888-950-5399

Authentic guaranteed memorabilia from all sports including NFL, MLB, NHL, NCAA, NASCAR, golf, boxing, tennis, AFL, minor league baseball.

Shipping: Free on orders over $50 or choose at checkout
Return Policy: Contact customer service within 30 days for RMA# - 15% restocking fee applies.
Payment Options: Major credit cards, PayPal, Bill Me Later

Similar sites:

www.sportsmemorabilia.com

1-800-689-2001

Shipping: Flat rate $4.99 on all orders
Return Policy: Contact customer service for RMA# - shipping and restocking fee applies.
Payment Options: Major credit cards, Google Checkout, PayPal

www.authenticsports.com

1-888-537-5656

Shipping: Free on orders over $100 or choose at checkout
Return Policy: Contact customer service within 15 days for RMA#
Payment Options: Major credit cards, PayPal, Google Checkout

SPORTS SHOES & APPAREL

www.onlinesports.com
1-800-856-2638

Sports and recreation products, shoes, apparel, memorabilia for every sport that you can think of.

Shipping: Choose at checkout
Return Policy: Contact customer service within 60 days for RMA#
Payment Options: Major credit cards

www.eastbay.com
1-800-826-2205

Great source for athletic footwear and apparel for men, women and kids at good prices – trainers starting at $9.99.

Shipping: Choose at checkout
Return Policy: Within 90 days
Payment Options: Major credit cards and PayPal

Similar Site:

www.roadrunnersports.com
1-800-743-3206

Shipping: Free
Return Policy: Contact customer service within 30 days
Payment Options: Major credit cards

www.finishline.com

1-800-777-3934

Shipping: Choose at chckout
Return Policy: Contact customer service within 45 days for RMA#
Payment Options: major credit cards

SPORTS RESULTS AND BLOGS

These sites give sports results and blog about sports.

www.skysports.com

www.nbcsports.com

www.oleole.com

www.playerpress.com

www.sportsblogs.com

www.deadspin.com

www.everydayshouldbesaturday.com

SWIMWEAR

www.swimoutlet.com

1-800-691-4065

Swimoutlet.com has clearance prices on swimwear for men, women and kids, as well as accessories for scuba gear, water aerobics, water polo, water shoes, sandals and much more.

Shipping: Free on orders over $75 or choose at checkout
Return Policy: Go online within 30 days of order to get RMA#. Must be in original unused condition.
Payment Options: Major credit cards

www.swimsuitsforall.com

1-888-241-7946

This "size 8 and up" site features women's sizes 8-16, plus sizes to 24W and maternity swimsuits.

Shipping: Choose at checkout
Return Policy: Return within 20 days in original unused condition with original tags. No returns on clearance items.
Payment Options: Major credit cards

TENNIS

www.tennisboom.com

1-800-336-8180

Racquets, strings, shoes, balls, bags, apparel and accessories for tennis, racquetball, badminton and squash. Many high end brands, and closeout and special sales sections.

Shipping: Free on orders over $99.99 or choose at checkout
Return Policy: 30 days in original condition
Payment Options: Major credit cards

TRAVEL

TRAVEL

These travel sites search out the best online deals on flights, hotels, cars, vacation packages and cruises based on your destination and dates of travel:

www.Kayak.com
1-203-899-3100

www.Expedia.com
1-800-397-3342

www.Orbitz.com
1-888-656-4546

www.Travelocity.com
1-888-872-8356

www.Bestfares.com
1-800-576-1700

www.Cheapoair.com
1-866-636-9088

www.Priceline.com
1-800-777-2354

www.Sidestep.com
1-203-899-3100

www.lastminutetravel.com

1-866-999-8942

www.farecompare.com

1-972-782-9249

www.cfares.com

1-650-620-1119

TRAVEL INSURANCE

The following are comparison sites to find the best rates for travel insurance so that you are covered anywhere in the world for your loss of luggage, health problems and delays:

- www.squaremouth.com
- www.quotewright.com
- www.insuremytrip.com
- www.travelguard.com
- www.tripinsurancestore.com
- www.totaltravelinsurance.com
- www.moneysupermarket.com
- www.accessamerica.com
- www.travelsafe.com
- www.moneysavingexpert.com

USEFUL TRAVEL SITES

The following are sites with useful information in their own way when planning any travel:

www.tripadvisor.com
1-617-670-6300

Site to help you plan your trip with reviews from over 20,000,000 travelers. For hotels and destinations. Loads of info and planner for your perfect trip.

www.igoyougo.com
1-212-372-5117

Reviews and recommendations from other travelers, sharing their experiences and photos. They also have travel deals.

www.flyfirstclass.com
1-800-883-5937

Flyfirstclass.com shows you how to save 40%-70% on business and first class airline tickets.

www.triporama.com
1-415-977-0209

Allows you to book group or family travel and share it all online with your traveling companions, discuss places to go and map the itinerary.

www.unusualhotelsoftheworld.com

via email

This web site has just what it says, unique, unusual and spe-cialty properties. Stay in an igloo in Canada, a lighthouse in the Netherlands, a tree house hotel in Sweden, a floating boathouse hotel in Canada, a caboose and carriages in New Zealand and much more. Worth going on just to see what they have. Great photos and details.

www.SeatGuru.com

1-617-670-6300

SeatGuru.com provides the consumer with a seat map graphic for each airline, together with in-depth seat-spe-cific comments denoting limited recline, reduced legroom, misaligned windows, emergency exits, power points, lava-tory, galley, etc. The seats are color coded on the map to help identify superior and substandard seats, so you can be totally informed when booking your seat.

www.realtravel.com

via email

Another highly-rated site that helps you plan your trip with advice and reviews from real travelers. Blogs and photos from other holidaymakers. They also have links to the latest deals.

www.dogfriendly.com

1-877-475-2275

This site publishes worldwide pet travel guides and requirements for dogs of all shapes and sizes. Includes pet-friendly hotels and details of flying overseas with information on customs and quarantine.

WOMEN

CLOTHES

www.fashionbug.com
1-888-273-3447

A wide selection of misses, junior and plus-sized women's clothing at excellent prices. Brands include Gitano, Studio 1940 and L.A. Blues.

Shipping: Choose at checkout
Return Policy: Within 90 days in original condition. Return slip enclosed in order.
Payment Method: Major credit cards

www.christopherandbanks.com
1-800-890-9601

christopherandbanks.com sells very reasonable women's clothes from $9.99 and up. Bottoms, tops, jackets, sweaters, dresses, skirts, pants and accessories.

Shipping: Choose at checkout
Return Policy: Within 60 days in original condition.
Payment Method: Major credit cards

Similar sites:

www.metrostyle.com

1-800-288-4000

Shipping: Choose at checkout
Return Policy: Within 60 days of purchase. Return slip in order.
Payment Method: Major credit cards

www.6pm.com

1-888-676-2660

Shipping: Choose at checkout
Return Policy: Go on website within 30 days and follow instructions
Payment Options: Major credit cards and Bill Me Later

LINGERIE

www.barenecessities.com

1-877-728-9272

Bras, panties, chemises, hosiery and accessories from brand names like Calvin Klein, La Perla, Wolford, Elle Macpherson Intimates and Spanx. Also has underwear and lounge pants for men including Calvin Klein and Polo.

Shipping: Choose at checkout
Return Policy: 60 days. 100% guarantee on unopened items. Return slip in order.
Payment Options: Major credit cards and Bill Me Later

PLUS SIZE CLOTHES

www.silhouettes.com

1-888-651-8337

Great fashions starting at size 12W. Tops, bottoms, jackets, pants, skirts, outerwear, special occasion, shoes and accessories.

Shipping: Choose at checkout.
Return Policy: Return within 90 days. Return slip in order.
Payment Options: Major credit cards.

www.onestopplus.com

1-800-400-4481

An online mall for plus sizes selling various top quality companies like Woman Within, Avenue, Chadwick and more. Apparel, lingerie, sleepwear, shoes and accessories. Sizes 12W-44W. Men's big and tall section features Chaps and Wrangler.

Shipping: Choose at checkout
Return Policy: Contact customer service within 90 days. Unused.
Payment Options: Major credit cards.

www.torrid.com
1-866-867-7431

For the thin at heart! Trendy "Diva-Style" plus-sized cloth-ing including Source of Wisdom and Z. Cavaricci Jeans, Ed Hardy tees and boots and fun costume jewelry.

Shipping: Choose at checkout
Return Policy: Contact customer service within 45 days. Some exclusions.
Payment Method: Major credit cards

www.cjbanks.com
1-800-890-9603

cjbanks.com has women's size 14W plus for tops, bottoms, denim, jackets, dresses, skirts and accessories.

Shipping: Choose at checkout
Return Policy: Within 60 days of purchase. Return slip in order.
Payment: Major credit cards

www.catherines.com
1-866-886-4720

Classic career and casual clothing for plus size women.

Shipping: free on $50 or more or choose online
Return Policy: Within 90 days – return slip in order
Payment Method: Major credit cards

LINGERIE

www.aboutcurves.com

1-877-287-8963

Lovely lingerie for plus size ladies to celebrate their curves.

Shipping: Choose at checkout
Return Policy: Some exceptions. Check with customer service and to get RMA#.
Payment Options: Major credit cards, PayPal.

SHOES

www.shoesteal.com

via email

This site is dedicated to discount shoe shoppers with shoes for women, men and kids, and many brand names including Michael Kors, Adidas, Crocs and more. Search by size, style, brand, color and price.

Shipping: Flat rate of $5 or choose at checkout
Return Option: Within 60 days – return label on back of original invoice.
Payment Options: Major credit cards

www.endless.com

1-866-218-9936

Designer shoes from Marc Jacobs, Kenneth Cole, Bally and dozens more all at 100% price guarantee.

Shipping: Free overnight
Return Policy: Return within 365 days unworn in original packaging.
Payment Options: Major credit cards

Similar sites:

www.shoes.com
via email

Shipping: Free ground or choose at checkout.
Return Policy: Return form online. Free returns.
Payment Options: Major credit cards, Bill Me Later, PayPal.

www.shoetrader.com
1-866-210-2664

Shipping: Free or choose at checkout
Return Policy: In original condition. Return slip in package
Payment Options: Major credit cards

www.onlineshoes.com
1-800-786-3141

Shipping: Choose at checkout
Return Policy: Within 90 days. Print return label online.
Payment Options: Major credit cards

WIGS AND HAIRPIECES

www.wowwigs.com

1-866-969-9447

Many style wigs and hairpieces for either fashion of costume.

Shipping: Free on orders over $49.95 or choose at checkout
Return Policy: No returns
Payment Options: Major credit cards and PayPal

Similar site:

www.beautytrends.com

1-800-268-7210

Shipping: Choose at checkout
Return Policy: Return within 60 days if unused only. Return slip in original package.
Payment Options: Major credit cards

WEDDINGS

BRIDAL GOWNS & BRIDESMAIDS OUTFITS AND SHOES

www.weddingdressdiscount.com

1-877-225-3685

weddingdressdiscount.com sells designer quality wedding gowns with savings of up to 80% off retail prices. Also available are bridesmaids dresses and accessories like garters, ring pillows and more.

Shipping: As requested
Return Policy: No returns
Payment: Major credit cards

www.houseofbrides.com

1-800-395-1240

Over 20,000 dresses for the bride, bridesmaid and mother of the bride, including many well-known designer names. Also available are shoes, lingerie and many, many accessories.

Shipping: As requested
Return Policy: No returns
Payment: Major credit cards and PayPal

www.maximumwoman.com
1-416-767-7007

Specializing in plus size dresses for special occasions – bride, bridesmaid, mother of the bride, plus accessories, jewelry and shoes, all at affordable prices.

Shipping: Choose at checkout
Return Policy: Some exclusions, contact customer service
Payment: Major credit cards

www.destinationweddingwear.com
1-858-605-1500

Custom-made bridal gowns at great prices, bridesmaid dresses and accessories for tropical weddings.

Shipping: Choose at checkout
Return Policy: Must contact customer service within 14 days for RMA#. Some exceptions apply.
Payment Options: Major credit cards

BRIDAL SHOES

www.bridalshoes.com
1-866-933-7463

Hundreds of styles of shoes including dyeables, flip flops, boots, ballerina and more, plus accessories and prom wear.
Shipping: Choose at checkout
Return Policy: Within 14 days. Return slip in order.
Payment Options: Major credit cards

Similar site:

www.onlinebridalstore. com
1-800-761-0176

Shipping: Free on orders over $30 or choose at checkout
Return Policy: Unused within 30 days. Restocking fee may apply.
Payment Options: Major credit cards

www.dyeablesshoes.com
1-888-434-4488

Shipping: Free
Return Policy: Unused within 30 days. Restocking fee of $6 applies
Payment Options: Major credit cards

HONEYMOON REGISTRY

www.honeymoonwishes.com

1-877-699-5884

On honeymoonwishes.com the bride and groom register for their honeymoon – the flight, the hotel and everything that goes with the trip. Family, friends and wedding guests can then go onto the site and choose what they would like to give as a wedding gift – so they can pay as little or as much as they like from a bottle of wine to a day sightseeing trip.

www.myregistry.com

via email

A global gift registry. Fill out your wish list from any store in the world and they will deliver it. Let your wedding guests shop from home.

www.giftregistrylocator.com

via email

Don't know where the couple is registered? Just put in a name, month and year of the wedding and the details of their registry comes up. Also track baby shower registries here.

USEFUL WEDDING WEBSITES

www.weddingwire.com
via email

Weddingwire.com is a wedding planner site – you put in your city and what you are looking for – from venue to cake to musicians – and they come up with a list in your area.

www.eweddingcake.com

Can't decide what sort of wedding cake you want? This site has pictures of hundreds of cakes, recipes, cake toppers and includes price guidelines and cake-cutting etiquette tips.

www.annsbridalbargains.com
1-800-821-7001

Keep the prices low without sacrificing the quality and service. Invitations, favors, napkins, decorations, stationery and accessories.

Shipping: Choose at checkout.
Return Policy: Contact customer service – some exceptions
Payment Options: Major credit cards and Bill Me Later

www.invitationsbykarina.com

1-888-4324002

Choose your invitation by theme and get a 30% discount off regular retail price.

Shipping: Choose at checkout
Return Policy: No returns as special order
Payment Options: Major credit cards

USEFUL WEBSITES

AIRPORT PARKING

Find the best deal for short or long-term airport parking in dozens of cities:

www.airportparkingreservations.com

www.parkrideflyusa.com

www.rideflyreservations.com

www.discountairportparking.com

www.fasttrack.com

www.airportparkingconnection.com

APARTMENT AND HOME RENTALS

Looking for a place to live or a vacation rental? These sites will help you find a rental apartment or house in no time. Put in your area and needs, like number of bedrooms and price, and what's available will come up for you to see.

www.rent.com

www.apartments.com

www.rentalhouse.com

www.move.com

www.findrentals.com

www.rentals.com

www.apartmentguide.com

www.houserentals.us

www.greatrentals.com

AUCTION WEBSITES

www.eBay.com

eBay.com is the largest and most well-known online auction website in the world for any and all items you might want to buy or sell.

Other similar sites:

www.eBids.com

www.uBid.com

www.amazonmarketplace.com

www.onlineauction.com

www.auction-warehouse.com

www.loot.com

www.gumtree.com

www.CQout.com

www.4sale4now.com

www.ePier.com

www.WeBidz.com

www.shopgoodwill.com

www.auctionfire.com

www.bidalot.com

www.itsgottago.com

www.auctionaddict.com

www.skyauction.com

www.gsaauction.com

www.auctionguide.com

www.auctionweiser.com

www.tazbar.com

www.InterBid.com

www.liquidation.com

www.fantasticbid.com

AUTO INSURANCE

The following are comparison sites for auto insurance:

www.insurance.com

www.esureance.com

www.autoinsurancequote.com

www.onlineautoinsurance.com

www.netquote.com

www.comparisonmarket.com

www.isure.com

www.carinsurance.com

www.pricingcentral.com

www.einsurancemarket.com

AUTO LEASING

The following are comparison sites for auto leasing:

www.pricequotes.com

www.carleasingsecrets.com

www.theleasingdirectory.com

www.automotive.com

www.leasecompare.com

www.takemypayments.com

www.leasetips.com

www.swapalease.com

www.edmunds.com

AUTO PRICES

The following are comparison sites for new and used car prices:

www.edmunds.com

www.carprice.com

www.kbb.com

www.pricequotes.com

www.priceshopping.com

www.carpricesecrets.com

www.carsdirect.com

www.autosite.com

www.usedcars.com

www.automotive.com

BANK RATES

The following are comparison sites to find the best bank rates for mortgages, credit cards, auto loans, CDs, retirement accounts and more.

www.bankrate.com

www.bankaholic.com

www.cdrates.com

www.moneyaisle.com

www.banx.com

www.moneyextra.com

www.findabetterbank.com

www.mortgagemarvel.com

www.banxquote.com

DOWNLOADABLE BOOKS

www.ebooks.com

via email

ebooks.com offers over 100,000 books that you can download to your computer, PDA or mobile phone. Best sellers at 10% discount off retail price.

www.booksonboard.com

via email

A similar site offering the same as e-books.com.

The following sites have free public domain e-books to download:

www.fictionwise.com

www.getfreebooks.com

www.manybooks.net

www.memoware.com

BROADBAND/CABLE/DSL DEALS

The following are comparison sites to find the best deals for Broadband, DSL or Cable in your area:

www.buytelco.com

www.dsldealfinder.com

www.moneysupermarket.com/broadband/

www.broadbandinfo.com

www.dslone.net

www.getcabledeals.com

BUSINESS INSURANCE

The following are comparison sites to find the best insurance rates for your business:

www.newinsurance.com

www.business.com

www.2insure4less.com

www.netquote.com

www.insurestop.com

www.coverzones.com

www.mostchoice.com

www.insurance-quote-us.com

www.insurancematch.com

www.4freequotes.com

www.partnersinsurance.com

CAR RENTAL COMPARISSON

The following are comparison sites to find the best car rentals in your area:

www.carrentalexpress.com

www.comparecarrental.com

www.priceline.com

www.kayak.com

www.compareoptions.com

www.my3cents.com

www.rentalcars.com

www.comparecarrentalsnow.com

www.carrentals.com

www.comparisontravel.com

www.sidestep.com

CELL PHONE PLANS

The following are comparison sites to find the best cell phone plans:

www.myrateplan.com

www.letstalk.com

www.consumercellular.com

www.billshrink.com

www.younevercall.com

www.cell-phone-plans.net

www.wirelessguide.com

www.phonedog.com

www.mobileburn.com

www.smarter.com

CHARITY

These sites enable you to help various charities without having to actually spend money! Use a search engine or bookmark sites for a "daily click" and your chosen charity benefits.

www.goodsearch.com

Use this site as a search engine when you surf the Internet and about a penny is donated to your favorite charity for every search.

www.goodshop.com

This partner site to goodsearch.com is an online shopping mall of world class merchants. Each purchase made via this mall will result in a donation to a charity that you designate, averaging approximately 3% of the sale. You'll also find coupons and discounts.

www.greatergood.com

This site is the Greater Good Network of websites. You choose the site you want to help from 'The Hunger Site', 'The Breast Cancer Site', The Rainforest Site', 'The Child Healthcare Site', 'The Animal Rescue Site', 'The Ecology Fund Site', or 'The Greater Good Site'.

If you just click on the 'click to give' area each day the sponsor advertisers on the site contribute to the charity.

Similar Charity sites based on the click idea:

www.oneclickatatime.org

www.charityclickdonation.com

www.thehungersite.com

www.dogpile.com

CLASSIFIED ADS

Below are sites for local classified ads – jobs, house hunting, goods, services, local activities and more. You can advertise something you have to offer or go onto the ads already listed for something you need.

www.craigslist.com

www.hobbly.com

www.domesticsale.com

www.webleeg.com

www.backpage.com

www.websbestclassifieds.com

www.classifieds.myspace.com

www.classifieds.yahoo.com

www.traderonline.com

www.hot-ads.com

www.freeclassifiedadsonline.com

www.salespider.com

COMPARISON DISCOUNT SHOPPING WEBSITES

The following are comparison websites for discount and free information on millions of products and merchandise:

www.pricescan.com

www.smartbargains.com

www.nextag.com

www.shopzilla.com

www.bizrate.com

www.pricegrabber.com

www.shopping.com

www.mysimon.com

www.dealtime.com

www.dealsnews.com

www.pricespider.com

www.dealsourcedirect.com

www.planetbargains.com

www.pricecomparison.com

www.smarter.com

www.pricecentral.com

www.coolshopping.com

www.shopping.yahoo.com

www.roboshopper.com

www.pricescan.com

www.shopper.cnet.com

www.search.live.com

www.google.com/products

www.bargain-predator.com

www.gearapalooza.com

www.buytrusted.com

www.yahooshopping.com

www.pronto.com

COUPONS AND WEEKLY DISCOUNTS

These are websites with coupons and weekly discounts, including local Sunday newspaper advertisements:

www.dealnews.com

www.dealalerter.com

www.bargainist.com

www.retailmenot.com

www.bestonlinecoupons.com

www.slickdeals.com

www.fatwallet.com

www.couponcabin.com

www.slickdeals.net

www.sundaysaver.com

www.salescircular.com

www.shoplocal.com

www.dealcatcher.com

www.sundaysaver.com

www.couponmountain.com

www.findsavings.com

www.couponalbum.com

www.dealstop.com

www.coolsavings.com

www.wow-coupons.com

www.flamingworld.com

www.allonlinecoupons.com

www.couponshack.com

www.couponwinner.com

www.couponcactus.com

www.greatcoupons-online.com

www.couponsdealspromos.com

www.dealio.com

www.couponmom.com

www.smartsource.com

www.couponcraze.com

www.keycode.com

www.refundsweepers.com

www.dealsofday.com

www.deallocker.com

www.simplybestcoupons.com

www.mycoupons.com

www.ultimatecoupons.com

CREDIT CARDS

The following are comparison sites for credit cards deals and rates:

www.creditcards.com

www.moneysupermarket.com

www.creditcardguide.com

www.cardratings.com

www.bankrate.com

www.creditorweb.com

www.bestcreditoffers.com

www.lowcards.com

CURRENCY CONVERTERS

Check the exchange rate before you travel:

www.xe.com

www.ratesfx.com

www.x-rates.com

www.advfn.com

DISCOUNT CODES

The following websites give codes for various retail websites. When you checkout there is a box for a promotional code – these sites give you those codes:

www.promotionalcodes.com

www.couponcodes4u.com

www.discountcodes.com

www.currentcodes.com

www.keycode.com

www.shoppersresource.com

www.couponcabin.com

www.couponcode.com

www.couponcodesonline.com

www.findsavings.com

www.addcoupons.com

www.digitaleditor.com

www.naughtycodes.com

www.couponmountain.com

FILE SHARE AND SWAP SITES

Below are file swap sites:

www.filesanywhere.com

www.fileswap.com

www.datamotion.com

www.file-swap.com

www.keepandshare.com

www.rapidshare.com

www.megaupload.com

www.egnyte.com

www.sendspace.com

www.zeropaid.com

www.sharefile.com

www.zeropaid.com

www.rapidshare.com

www.trueshare.com

www.mediafire.com

www.foldershare.com

www.docstoc.com

www.windowslinskydrive.com

www.mybloop.com

FILTERING SOFTWARE

Here are some sites with software to protect your kids on the internet especially with the influx of social networking sites:-

www.cybersitter.com

www.cyberpatrol.com

www.netnanny.com

www.softforyou.com

FREE SAMPLES AND FREE STUFF

These are websites with free downloads and free stuff:

www.thefreebiesource.com

www.simplyfreesamples.com

www.freesampleforager.com

www.missfreebie.com

www.thunderfap.com

www.thefreesite.com

www.all-free-samples.com

www.welovefreebies.com

www.freefusion.net

www.coolfreebielinks.com

www.freakyfreddies.com

www.killerfreebies.com

www.freestuffchannel.com

www.heyitsfree.com

www.gotofreestuff.com

www.top20free.com

www.bestfreestuffonline.com

www.thefreesite.com

www.freeflys.com

www.bargainsavingsnetwork.com

www.ilovefreethings.com

www.yourfunfreestuff.com

HOME EXCHANGE

Below are sites to help you exchange your home for another anywhere in the world:

www.homeexchange.com

www.ltamos.com

www.onlinehousetrading.com

www.homelink-usa.com

www.tradetotravel.com

www.homeforexchange.com

www.1sthomeexchange.com

www.homeforhome.com

www.exchangehomes.com

HEALTH INSURANCE

The following are comparison sites to find the best rates and plans for your health insurance:

www.ehealthinsurance.com

www.healthinsurancefinders.com

www.netquote.com

www.bestratelifehealth.com

www.thehealthquote.com

www.healthinsurance.com

www.4freequotes.com

www.insureco.org

INTERNET SUPERSTORES

www.overstock.com

via-email

Overstock.com is an online retail department store with quality merchandise from many leading brand-name companies at significant discounts.

Shipping: Flat rate of $2.95 or choose at checkout.
Return Policy: On site to your account to get return label. 20% restocking fee applies.
Payment Options: Major credit cards, PayPal, Bill Me Later, money orders.

www.classiccloseouts.com

via-email

Clothing for men, women and kids, home accessories, jewelry, health and beauty and more. Plus added discounts in their bargain bin.

Shipping: Free on orders over $40 or choose at checkout
Return Policy: Go onto site to customer service within 30 days for RMA#
Payment Options: Major credit cards and PayPal

www.buy.com

via email

Great brand names at great prices ranging from computer hardware and software, cell phones, books, movies, sporting goods, music and more.

Shipping: Choose at checkout
Return Policy: Go on site to your account and get RMA#
Payment Options: Major credit cards, PayPal, Google Checkout, eBillMe, Google Checkout, Bill Me Later.

www.unbeatablesale.com

1-888-657-8436

Electronics, furniture, baby products, housewares, kitchen, sports, garden, toys, games and more.

Shipping: Free on some items or choose at checkout
Return Policy: Contact customer service within 30 days for RMA#. Shipping costs and 25% restocking fee applies.
Payment Options: Major credit cards and PayPal

www.dealyard.com

1-866-320-3325

Dealyard.com sells a variety of products ranging from kitchen appliances, faucets, electric blankets, ipod accessories, small electronics and much more.

Shipping. Choose at checkout
Return Policy: Must contact customer service within 7 days for RMA#. Restocking fee of 15% applies
Payment Options: Major credit cards and PayPal

JOB SEARCH

These sites are for all aspects of employment including entry level, temp work, government employment and volunteer work:

www.freecareersearch.com

www.monster.com

www.careerbuilder.com

www.simplyhired.com

www.craigslist.org

www.yahoohotjobs.com

www.job.com

www.truecareers.com

www.dice.com

www.collegerecruiter.com

www.jobcentral.com

www.nettemps.com

www.linkedin.com

www.alljobsearch.com

www.indeed.com

www.truecareers.com

www.usajobs.gov

www.careerjournal.com

www.jobbankinfo.org

www.directemployer.com

www.employmentwizard.com

www.healthyjobsstarthere.com

www.careerjet.com

www.computerjobs.com

www.idealist.org

www.mediabistro.com

www.worktree.com

www.wetfeet.com

www.6figurejobs.com

www.job-hunt.org

LANGUAGE TRANSLATORS

The following websites will translate text that you enter into other languages for free:

www.appliedlanguage.com

www.translation2.paralink.com

www.worldlingo.com

www.freetranslation.com

www.google.com/language_tools

LEGAL SERVICES

www.legalzoom.com

1-888-791-0227

A quick and affordable service to get legal help with common legal matters like drafting a will or trust, incorporating a business, divorce, trademarks and copyrights.

Similar sites:

www.legaldocumentfinder.com

www.legalhelpmate.com

www.legalhelper.com

www.legalcpu.com

LIFE INSURANCE

The following are comparison sites to find the best rates and plans for your life insurance:

www.intelliquote.com

www.accuquote.com

www.selectquote.com

www.insurance.com

www.insure.com

www.efinancial.com

www.wholesaleinsurance.net

MORTGAGE RATES

The following are comparison sites to find the best rates and plans that suit your needs for a mortgage:

www.shoprate.com

www.quickenloan.com

www.bankrate.com

www.mortgagemarvel.com

www.mortgageloan.com

www.interest.com

www.freeratesearch.com

www.guaranteedrate.com

www.myhomemortgage.com

www.imortgageguide.com

PHOTO SHARING SITES

The following sites are for sharing your photos with family and friends or the world:

www.webshots.com

www.printroom.com

www.bluemelon.com

www.snapfish.com

www.flikr.com

www.fireworks.com

www.folki.com

www.dropshots.com

www.pixamo.com

www.picturetrail.com

www.dotphoto.com

www.slide.com

www.photobucket.com

www.smugmug.com

www.snappages.com

www.pbase.com

www.jumpcut.com

REAL ESTATE VALUATIONS

If you decide you want to sell your home these sites allow you to enter your address and come up with the approximate value of the house:

www.zillow.com

www.homegain.com

www.realestatevalues.com

www.homevaluehunt.com

www.free-home-appraisal.com

www.realestate.yahoo.com/homevalues

www.truilia.com

RECIPES

Below are websites that give you FREE recipes:

www.allrecipes.com

www.ichef.com

www.recipesource.com

www.epicurean.com

www.freerecipe.org

www.free-gourmet-recipes.com

www.recipegoldmine.com

www.cooking.com

www.jamieoliver.com

www.foodnetwork.com

www.foodchannel.com

www.recipestoday.com

www.epicurious.com

REFERENCE AND RESEARCH SITES

Support sites for students and professionals looking to research anything and everything:

www.wikipedia.com

www.britannica.com

www.about.com

www.dictionary.com

www.archive.org

www.WebMD.com

www.usa.gov

www.A9.com

www.publiclibraries.com

www.consumersearch.com

www.answers.com

www.google.com

www.itools.com

RENTERS INSURANCE

The following are comparison sites to find the best rates and plans if you are renting an apartment or house and need to cover your personal property:

www.rentersinsurance.com

www.insurestop.com

www.myrateplan.com

www.insureme.com

www.ensurance.com

www.pricescan.com

www.youcovered.com

www.hometownquotes.com

www.insurancesalesman.com

www.erenterplan.com

www.einsurancemarket.com

www.affordablehomeinsurance.com

SCREEN SAVERS

Free Screen Savers to download:

www.screensavers.com

www.free-downloadable-software.com

www.acez.com

www.screensavers4fun.com

www.screensaversforpc.com

www.screensaversgallery.com

www.popularscreensavers.com

www.screensaverfree.com

www.4-freescreensavers.com

www.topscreensavers4free.com

www.aaascreensavers.com

SEARCH ENGINES

Below are the most popular search engines on the Internet:

www.google.com

www.yahoo.com

www.ask.com

wwwa.askjeeves.com

www.altavista.com

www.alltheweb.com

www.excite.com

www.aol.com

www.hotbot.com

www.superpages.com

www.lycos.com

www.mamma.com

www.opendirectory.com

www.webcrawler.com

www.gigablast.com

www.munkey.com

www.exalead.com

www.surfwax.com

www.clusty.com

www.infomine.com

www.leapfish.com

SHIPPING RATES

The following are useful sites for comparison shipping rates throughout the world:

www.shippingsidekick.com

www.shipgoods.com

www.shippingquotes.org

www.iship.com

www.shipgooder.com

www.shipwire.com

www.freightz.com

www.pakmail.com

SITTERS

Sites to find the perfect baby sitter, nanny, senior care or petsitter:

www.sittercity.com

www.findpetcare.com

www.babysitters4hire.com

www.nannies4hire.com

www.4nannies.com

www.seniordecision.com

SHOPPING CLUBS

www.qvc.com

1-800-367-9444

qvc.com is a worldwide shopping club and one of the largest multi-media retailers in the world. Items for sale include jewelry, fashion, beauty, kitchen items, electronics, goods for the home, wellness and sports, toys, leisure and craft.

Shipping: Choose at checkout
Returns: Return label with order and instructions
Payment: QVC Speedbuy, major credit cards and debit card with Visa or MasterCard.

www.samsclub.com

local #s online

No Sam's Club in your area? Join online and get great discounts on products including jewelry, designer goods, collectibles, electronics, apparel, floral and organic foods and meats.

Shipping: Choose at checkout
Return Policy: 100% guarantee return with receipt and unopened. Online return details on website.
Payment: Major credit cards, Discover Sams credit card, Debit Visa or MasterCard.

www.costco.com

1-800-955-2292

Costco.com is a membership club with varying levels of membership – the most expensive Executive membership receives a 2% rewards on most purchases. They sell food, wine, appliances, auto, bed and bath, books/CD's/DVD's, toys, games, computers, electronics and much more.
Shipping: Choose at checkout
Returns: Go on line or call to expedite
Payment: Costco Amex, Costco Cash Card only

SOCIAL NETWORKING SITES

The following are sites for social networking:

www.myspace.com

www.bebo.com

www.blogger.com

www.flickr.com

www.friendster.com

www.facebook.com

www.youtube.com

www.classmatesonline.com

www.livejournal.com

www.msnspaces.com

www.yahoo360.com

www.xanga.com

www.myyearbook.com

www.scribd.com

www.hi5.com

www.wordpress.com

www.sixapart.com

www.orkut.com

www.tagged.com

www.perfspot.com

www.zorpia.com

www.windowslivespace.com

www.ning.com

www.twitter.com

SWAP SITES FOR BOOKS, DVDs, CDs AND GAMES

www.bookmoosh.com

www.bookins.com

www.paperbackswap.com

www.swap.com

www.titletrader.com

www.swaptree.com

www.peerflix.com

www.lala.com

www.playinterchange.com

www.goozex.com

www.swapthing.com

www.swapacd.com

www.swapstation.com

www.swapyourgames.com

www.switchgames.com

www.gameswap.com

www.tradegamesnow.com

www.mrswap.com

www.estarland.com

www.secondspin.com

www.Qswap.com

www.spun.com

www.switchhouse.com

www.half.com

www.switchplanet.com

www.bookcrossing.com

GENERAL SWAP SITES

The following are swap sites that have become huge on the Internet. The idea is you can exchange or barter anything that you have and no longer want for something that you do want:

www.barterquest.com

www.mytradeamerica.com

www.swap.com

www.webswap.com

www.bigvine.com

www.swapace.com

www.trashbank.com

www.titletrader.com

www.neighborrow.com

www.intellibarter.com

www.zwaggle.com

www.swapathome.com

www.stashswap.com

www.swap-bot.com

www.itex.com

www.gimmeyourstuff.com

www.friendlyfavor.com

www.favorpals.com

www.u-exchange.com

UTILITIES

Get the best local deal with these two comparison sites

www.uswitch.com

www.moneysupermarket.com

and to go online and turn on your utilities go to:

www.whitefence.com

WEBHOSTING

Once you have put your website together here are FREE web-hosting sites:

www.homestead.com

www.atspace.com

www.150m.com

www.free.20m.com

www.50webs.com

www.freehostia.com

www.100webspace.com

www.awardspace.com

www.byethost.com

www.110mb.com

www.trap17.com

www.thepewesbite.com

WEBSITE TEMPLATES

These sites all have easy to use FREE templates for you to build a website:

www.webs.com

www.homeshead.com

www.freewebsitetemplates.com

www.freewebtemplates.com

www.freesitetemplates.com

www.freelayouts.com

www.easytemplates.com

www.freetemplatesonline.com

www.myfreetemplatehome.com

WEBSITE INDEX

www.ingramcontent.com/pod-product-compliance
Lightning Source LLC
Chambersburg PA
CBHW061000280326
41935CB00009B/777